T0209002

ON THE
OUTSKIRTS
OF HEAVEN

A NEAR-DEATH TALE OF SOUL RETRIEVAL

PEP TORRES

BALBOA.
PRESS

A DIVISION OF HAY HOUSE

Balboa Press books may be ordered through booksellers or by contacting:

Balboa Press
A Division of Hay House
1663 Liberty Drive
Bloomington, IN 47403
www.balboapress.com
1 (877) 407-4847

Because of the dynamic nature of the Internet, any web addresses or links contained in this book may have changed since publication and may no longer be valid. The views expressed in this work are solely those of the author and do not necessarily reflect the views of the publisher, and the publisher hereby disclaims any responsibility for them.

The author of this book does not dispense medical advice or prescribe the use of any technique as a form of treatment for physical, emotional, or medical problems without the advice of a physician, either directly or indirectly. The intent of the author is only to offer information of a general nature to help you in your quest for emotional and spiritual well-being. In the event you use any of the information in this book for yourself, which is your constitutional right, the author and the publisher assume no responsibility for your actions.

Any people depicted in stock imagery provided by Getty Images are models, and such images are being used for illustrative purposes only. Certain stock imagery © Getty Images.

Print information available on the last page.

ISBN: 978-1-9822-0691-8 (sc)
ISBN: 978-1-9822-0692-5 (hc)
ISBN: 978-1-9822-0693-2 (e)

Library of Congress Control Number: 2018907263

Balboa Press rev. date: 09/11/2018

CONTENTS

FOREWORD

More than twenty years ago, I was involved in a catastrophic auto accident in which my heart stopped, and I found myself on the outskirts of the afterlife, in a strange limbo I call the Boulevard of the Dead. What follows is the story of my near-death journey and a consideration of the life altering lessons learned there.

Whether a dream, trick of the mind, or a mental defense mechanism triggered to soften the transition between here and oblivion, I believe it was real. Whatever it was changed me forever, affirmed for me my mission in life and strengthened my faith in a divine other side.

I offer this tale of my white light moment to you as inspiration to pursue your own life's mission, as a reminder that our lives are mysterious blessings and as an affirmation that we are much more than we believe we are and that there is much more to our reality than we think there is.

It is also a call to arms, for revolution against evil and the sinister instruments of deception that block us from our creator and enslave our souls within a powerful illusion.

I should say, at this point, that this tale comes to you as a collaborative meditative effort between me and my guardian angel…

Indeed, it does. We worked together.

whoever that may turn out to be. His words, his interjections will always appear in **bold italicized print.** Sometimes he will come in a lot and other times he will come in only here and there.

Sometimes not at all.

Whenever and however he decides, I suppose.

As the spirit moves me.

There will even be times when we will engage in brief and thoughtful discourse as we tell our story.

We will also pause occasionally to highlight important lessons and to offer brief new insights in, what we will call, **The Old Painter's Gallery.**

This tale is true. I really was in a catastrophic accident, my heart really did stop, I really did die, and I did cross over to the other side, to a place I call the Boulevard of the Dead. My guardian angel, a strangely familiar gentleman dressed as a painter, really did appear to me in my car and it was he who guided me down that haunted street and reminded me of the true meaning and urgent purpose of my life.

Through me you would learn the ways of the Ghost Warrior and of the power of the Quetzal. I would open your eyes to the revolution that is coming, one you and a growing number of newly enlightened warriors are soon to join, maybe even lead.

Of course, my angel and I have engineered various enhancements here and there, whenever memory itself fails, so as to fill in some gaps in our story and to make sure that the lessons of that journey are better communicated. Still, the story is true.

And the message is urgent.

We are still in constant contact, my angel and me. As I have stated, we worked together, along with my jaguar nagual…

The jade jaguar…

…to co-author this humble work. Together, we recall events and make sense of all the lessons learned on that day… the day I died, reconnected with my soul, found my purpose then came back to life to paint the world blue.

Pep Torres

Me and My Pop

The day after my father passed away, I drove to one of my favorite spots, a cliff overlooking the Pacific in Santa Barbara, California, where I drew this picture. Today, this picture hangs above my art desk at home beside a photograph of my father in his prime.

PAINT THE WORLD BLUE

My father died in 1987. With his passing, I fell into a deep and horrible depression. That's not to say that I was even close to having my life together before my father died. It seemed that I had always been an emotional and financial mess. I was already a basket case in many ways. Whatever the root causes…

We certainly won't go into all of them in this book.

…I was drowning in my own desperation and drama. Pulling no punches, I was a painfully insecure, immature, shamefully self-indulgent twenty-something intent on cutting corners, avoiding responsibility, breaking rules and destroying myself.

It's no parent's dream to have someone as immature and as inexperienced as I was then influencing young minds in a classroom. I was just a big kid. Yet, there I was, fresh out of college, newly married then quickly divorced, doing the best I could as a teacher on an emergency credential. Later, I would be blessed with the opportunity to indulge my crazy passion for basketball by becoming a head varsity basketball coach at various California high schools.

With all humility, kids loved me. I was innately gifted in the classroom and on the court. Without the proper training, I was a natural. Instinctively, from day one, I knew how to engage my students, how to get them to listen and want to learn. While I was shy and reclusive outside my classroom, I was an outrageous ham within it, using all my natural talents as an actor, an artist and storyteller to capture the attention of my students so that I could teach and inspire them.

Inspire them?

To dream.

You were a mess of a person outside the classroom.

A total mess. I was, in the words of my one that got away girlfriend, "a beautiful basket case."

I come from a family of high achieving and talented people. My father was a world-famous dancer in the thirties and forties, my mother and step-father were Ranchera singing college professors and my sister was an Emmy award winning journalist on the Hollywood fast-track.

I, on the other hand, was a divorced 27-year-old man, blessed with a multitude of artistic and athletic talents, my father's choice to change the world, who somehow was never able to pull it all together, scraping along on a teacher's salary and living in a studio apartment.

I never did drugs and had no taste for booze; I was a gym rat, actually, spending all my free time there outside of work or the dark, safe and comfortable confines of my bedroom, pumping iron, playing basketball or watching movies.

Basketball and movies – your two great passions and diversions.

Don't forget food.

Ah, yes, the epic eating binges; decadent and messy affairs in which you disappeared into your darkened apartment for days so as to indulge your loneliness in front of the television set, with pizza, Big Gulps and chocolate.

Yes. I forgot that you were there.

Indeed.

My father's death hurt.

Naturally.

Along with the normal pain associated with the loss of a parent, there was a mountain of guilt attached to my grief.

When I was nine, my father, already a man of advanced years in his late sixties, foretold that I would forget and deny him.

"Someday," he told me, "you will be all grown up and you will be approached by an old man. He will say to you, 'Pep, Pep, don't you remember me?' You will look at him and say, 'I'm sorry, sir, but I don't know who you are.'"

I promised my father that would never happen, that I would never forget my daddy, who was my hero.

Forget him, however, you did. Deny him you did and trade him in for a younger, more active and adventurous father you did as well.

Yes and because of this, his death was so much more difficult to reconcile. In this state of guilt and despair, my life spiraled even further out of control. It was then that my best friend, Jake, came to me with a Christmas gift.

"There's a man in Tucson," he said, "a Medicine Man who changed my life and I know he can change yours."

He was quite powerful, this Medicine Man, and descended from a great lineage. In Tucson, he was a lead medicine man of the Comanche Nation and the director of the Native American division of a respected local hospital.

"He's running a weeklong seminar on Traditional Indian Medicine," Jake continued, "I think you should come."

I was reluctant.

"I'm not into that kind of stuff, Jake," I told him, "I'm not into cults."

"It's not like that," he answered, "no cults, Pep. People from all the healing professions will be there; doctors, nurses, counselors, and teachers, like us. They're coming from all over the world, man. Trust me."

Broke on a beginning teacher's salary, I couldn't afford the cost anyway. It was $500.00 for the week-long seminar and that didn't include food or lodging. For me, that was a lot.

"It's a gift, Pep," he said, "It's already paid for."

It was a gift that would change your life forever. Maybe not immediately, but eventually.

"It's better than locking yourself up in a dark room for three days," Jake continued, "with your pizza and Big Gulps!"

Jake knew you well.

So many wonderful things occurred that week, so many revelations about the nature of spirit and the divinity that connects us all. Here, I learned of ritual and of Rainbow Way Meditation.

Of these we will also talk more about.

In Tucson, I briefly reconciled my guilt over my father. Through guided meditations, he and Jake helped to release me from the shackles of my past, from my anger, my guilt. For an all too brief a time, I experienced what peace of mind could feel like.

For one week, your restless soul found a peace, a truth and a meaning it had never known and which, once you lost it, would take years to find again.

It was a harmony and focus I felt sure would follow me home, after the seminar. For a week I actually loved myself, not for anything I had achieved or earned but just because. I loved myself just because God loved me, because of the growing sense within me of my oneness with God. I had every expectation that this sense of oneness, this peace, would last forever.

It did not.

I lacked the discipline in the process of my own healing. The peace and oneness I was experiencing through guided meditations and counseling was a great start but the rest was supposed to be up to me, to my own initiative, my own guidance. Unfortunately, I wasn't looking to do work but, instead, looked to God, or some other outside force for a miracle, to do the work for me; a push button solution that would release me of the responsibility for undertaking the process of my own healing.

It was only a matter of days after returning from the seminar, to real life, that you relapsed into old self-destructive ways.

As if in rebellious response to any positive changes I made, I was worse than ever; more reckless, hopeless, impulsive and out of control. As a result, I was also more frustrated, more depressed and more hateful of myself than ever before.

This Medicine Man would often tell us that "Once you know better, you can't go back. Every time you make the same mistake over and over, the consequences become greater and greater." To be sure, after the seminar, I did know better and the consequences I would face for my self-destructive patterns, my impatience, the many dark self-indulgences, would soon take a heavy toll.

Heavier than you could ever have known.

Seven years later, after a series of unhealthy romances...

Wild times, amid which your soul mate, that 'one that got away,' flashed in and out of your life. You let her go...

So as not to hurt her.

You hurt her by letting her go.

This is not the time for that story...

Another book, I suppose. Still, she loved you and saw the best in you.

I didn't believe what she saw.

What is it Cassandra said?

Cassandra is my stepmother, my father's wife and widow.

She told you that the women you chose reflected the way you saw yourself. It would have been so much easier if you had been able to see yourself as your soul mate did.

I didn't like myself very much.

Obviously, leaving her behind deviated from the divine plan that both of you decided on in Heaven. The consequences for that would be...

Severe.

To be sure, I found myself in an even greater mess. Having already failed at marriage once, I found myself married yet again; this time to a much younger street savvy chick I didn't love with a baby on the way.

I was still mourning over my father, still working unsuccessfully through my guilt at not being there for him as he suffered through Alzheimer's Disease, as he called out for me on so many occasions; not being there for him on the day that he died.

Still broke and the sole provider of a family, I was now struggling to make a living as a teacher in the high-priced paradise of the Monterey Bay. I was still a beautiful basket case, still lost, desperate, lonely (despite being married), haunted by my own demons and smothered in my own drama, overwhelmed by my own karma. I prayed for a do over and it came suddenly on the road to Loma, a small California coastal town, early one foggy morning, on the corner of Beach and Main, the day I sped through an intersection into another dimension, onto the Boulevard of the Dead.

OLD PAINTER'S GALLERY 1

The old painter, my guardian angel, is very wise. As spirit, he observes life from a unique perspective. He knows many things about life and the universe.

Indeed I do.

He is not a scientist, a theologian or an expert on anything. He is an artist.

As are we all — each of us creating in our own unique ways.

Knowledge comes to him through the **Quetzal**, the light-sonic frequency of God, the greatest artist of all. The old painter is not all-knowing.

Like all of you, I can only interpret the knowledge within my own, admittedly limited, capacity to understand. While I have seen God's plan and my place in it, I lack the aptitude to fully grasp it all. What I am certain of is this; there is a plan and we have purpose within it.

With him, there are no big terms, no intricate and complicated explanations. Just the truth…

As I perceive it.

The Quetzal

The Quetzal is the light-sonic frequency of God. Some call it the God Frequency. It is within this divine vibration that God creates all things and through which God communicates with humanity and all living things. God communicates with us in many ways — many times, when we are sleeping, in our dreams. It is during deep sleep that consciousness is most naturally altered and when God slips into our dreams to deliver messages and reinforce our purpose in life with imagery to be decoded when we awake. It is in a state of sleep when many of us, unwittingly, connect with the Quetzal.

It is not only within our dreams that God communicates to us but also in the dreams we have for our lives. We all have dreams. We all have those great callings, those passions, the things we feel called to do with our lives - some dream of being writers; others dream about being actors, scientists, explorers, politicians, professional athletes; still, others dream of painting the world blue with the stories they tell.

It is important to know that these dreams we have for our lives, well…they're God too. Our passions are God's gift to us. Our dreams, our callings, those things we wish we could do are all God's way of letting us know, reminding us actually, what we are supposed to do with our lives – reminding us of our purpose and mission in life. God wants us to live out our dreams. It is God's will that we do. Our dreams are, in fact, divine mandates decided upon by us and God in the spirit world before we were born, when we forged the divine plans for our lives.

There are other ways, too, that God reaches out to us, working to get our attention, to guide and help us navigate the path of our divine plan. Throughout the day, God, the universe, communicates through various signs and synchronicities that serve as both validations and as calls to action. When we recognize these signs, we are expected to obey them. That takes knowing, faith. Only by connecting to the Quetzal can mankind truly free itself from the oppressive trappings of the material world – which we are soon to learn is but an illusion.

How, then, can we better connect with the Quetzal and become one with God and the Universe? Meditation is always a good start – finding a quiet spot where one can empty the mind of all the white noise so as to hear the voice of God.

This Comanche Medicine Man always knew that he would never prosper from his teachings, but he meant them to be shared with the world. Through this book, at least some of his teachings will be.

Conducive to meditation, and so often ignored, is a healthy lifestyle consisting of regular exercise and a predominantly plant-based diet.

RE-BIRTHDAY

On the first of October every year I celebrate my "re-birthday." That's the day I ran a red through a foggy intersection, a silver van colliding into the driver's side of my red Honda Civic at 45 mph. On that day, dressed in the same gray sweats that I used as pajamas, my heart stopped beating and I passed from this land of the living into a place I call the Boulevard of the Dead.

There were no dark dreams the night before, no signs, no omens, no funny Final Destination feelings of foreboding, absolutely no hints that I was going to die that morning.

It happened so quickly that the moment was not even perceived. I didn't even know it happened. I didn't even know that I died.

Some people say they see a white light when they die, I saw a red one. A traffic light. I still remember my wife, crying out my name as I approached that point of no return, darting past the crosswalk and into the intersection.

"Pep!" she cried out, yanking me out from whatever daze I had fallen into. It was yet another rough and stressful night for me. There were so many things on my mind that morning, so many pictures floating through my head: financial problems, job stress, a horribly unhappy marriage, and a baby on the way. I just zoned out. Not unlike a hundred other times in my life where I zoned out and couldn't figure later how I got from point A to B.

That's when angels take the wheel.

Only difference, this time, was that I never made it to point B.

"Pep!" she cried out again, our hyper miniature Doberman bouncing wildly about the car. First, I looked at her. Horrified, she stiffened, bracing for an impact. Then, I looked left to see a silver van coming hard upon us. All moved in slow motion as I pulled the wheel hard right then left, swerving a bit and taking air, dodging the van and narrowly avoiding disaster.

I was strangely euphoric, happily buzzed, as our Honda jettisoned safely through the intersection and proceeded down Main Street, into the heart of Loma, California, the last place on Earth I ever thought I would die.

But you did die.

We did not escape collision. Instead, and here I must rely on what I am told for I recall only what occurred along the Boulevard of the Dead, the silver van nailed us on my driver's side, smashing my left arm, which hung leisurely outside the window, crushing my ribs and shoulder, puncturing my lungs and stopping my heart.

The red Civic was really knocked off the road like a pinball; zig-zagging out of control until it came to a fuming rest, upside down and totaled, wedged between a cement light post and the wall of a Latino Music Store on the corner of Beach and Main.

Miraculously, my wife, who wasn't wearing a seatbelt came out of the whole mess with little more than bruises and some soreness the next day, the baby in her belly completely unharmed.

My wife must have been shocked to see me so lifeless and covered in blood. Try as she might, she could not revive me. Most important, she was also trapped in the smoldering wreckage and had to wait helplessly as the Jaws of Life split the car in fours to free her and allow paramedics to get to me.

From there, I was taken to Loma Community Hospital, where, unconscious, I was rushed to Emergency. I opened my eyes to see, blurry at first, the face of a young nurse tending to my facial wounds. Meanwhile, a male nurse pulled a shard of glass from my temple. I was so drugged up, I didn't even realize I was broken all over.

"You were in an accident," the young nurse said. Behind her stood, I thought, a familiar face, a little old man with a cap, looking over her shoulder.

That was me.

"My wife?" I asked.

"She's fine."

"My baby?"

"Fine"

"Was anybody hurt?"

"Only you."

You were all messed up.

"Am I going to be okay?" I asked, "Am I going to live?"

By this time, the old man was gone.

I was there, though. I was always there.

"I can't tell you that," she responded coldly, and, with that, I was stunned.

I don't remember the impact of the crash, the Jaws of Life, the paramedics or the ride to the hospital. I have no memories of what happened before I opened my eyes to that young nurse for I was somewhere else, separate from my body.

I do, however, have vivid memories of another place, of an ethereal journey that didn't end at that intersection but began there. A place where several familiar ghosts, or spirits…

Maybe, angels or even God in forms you'd be most receptive to.

…met me at various stops along that road, to guide me to redemption and remind me of my identity, my purpose, my divinity and to prepare me I believe for greater things…

Revolution.

…for a life as a…Ghost Warrior.

Allow me to share all that I remember of my journey through the Boulevard of the Dead…

Allow us to share…

…and, in that, free your spirit and inspire within you a sense of your own purpose, identity and a faith that all things dreamed are meant to be lived.

BOULEVARD OF THE DEAD

I didn't know I was dead, I had no knowledge of the chaos erupting at the corner of Beach and Main; the screams, the sirens or crowds that gathered about my wrecked car, my mangled body, lifeless and bloody, my pregnant wife crying for me to open my eyes. I wasn't there and, wherever I was, I thought I had avoided disaster and dodged death altogether.

I remember shooting through the intersection into a mist-soaked street, regaining control of my car and finding myself within a whirling neon funnel of blue fog. Through this glimmering blue mist, I could see the hazy blur of streetlamps on the sidewalks and lights of little shops lining the boulevard. I was so light of mind, it didn't even dawn on me that my wife was no longer sitting beside me. I was just driving in the moment, driving without question, I wasn't coming from, or going to, anywhere.

The Old Painter

"Heaven," I thought, in wonder of the glowing blue fog and by the sense of harmony now overflowing within me.

"Almost," a gravelly voice answered my thought, "not quite."

I turned to see a wrinkled old man smiling at me from the passenger seat.

That was me.

Yes, you looked very old, at least ninety, your weathered face a crumpled mesh of deeply etched crisscrossing lines. This old painter wore an old brown cap, much like the one I myself have been known to wear, atop a thick mop of long gray hair and was dressed in old paint-splotched overalls. Paint brushes of various bristle widths stuck out from his pockets and at his feet were two buckets of paint, labeled, "Blue."

Although I couldn't place this old painter, he seemed very familiar to me and his presence was somehow reassuring.

"Keep your eyes on the road," he said with a twinkle in his eye, "wouldn't want to get in an accident, would we?"

He was delighted by his own wit and I recognized his loud, whole-hearted laughter. As he laughed, he slapped his bony knee. There was a brown mole on the top of his left hand, between his thumb and forefinger, the same mole that both my father and I had on our hands.

Tightening my grip on the wheel, I squinted as I strained to see through the fog and keep my focus on the road. Here and there, wherever the fog broke, I saw the hazy jade colored outline of a giant cat of prey racing alongside my car.

That was your jaguar nagual, your power animal. Like me, he has always watched over you as a kind of angel. Your jaguar would facilitate our journey through the Boulevard of the Dead, unlocking dimensional doorways leading to Heaven. Though you would not always see him, he was protecting us from evil the whole time.

"Who are you?" I asked.

"Keep driving," the old painter directed.

"Where are we going? I asked.

I was so mesmerized by this foggy blue limbo that I could care less actually where we were going. I was content to lose myself in the fog and might have cruised drunkenly down that murky road for eternity if not for the lighthearted distraction of this comical old painter.

"To the end of this boulevard," he answered, motioning forward with a shriveled hand. I looked through the windshield but couldn't see to the end of the street. The fog was too thick.

"The drive will give us time to talk," he said, "and reacquaint ourselves."

"Do you know me?"

He nodded.

"Do I know you?" I asked.

He nodded.

I'd been with you from the start, from before you were born, in Heaven, when you chose this life. I, and your nagual, have always tried to guide you, to keep you on track; whispering in your ear, coming to you in dreams, constantly showing you signs. You wouldn't look or listen. You ignored us.

I remembered him now, this old painter. It came to me suddenly. He appeared to me often in my dreams when I was a child.

I thought it would be easier to reach you in your dreams. We thought, the jaguar and I, that you would feel less threatened by us.

That's how I knew you.

This old painter haunted me when I couldn't sleep, his dark shadow, along with that of a giant cat of prey, appearing on my bedroom wall in the middle of the night. It was his deep laugh, almost like my father's laugh or even my own, I heard at night when everyone else was sleeping and his voice that whispered my name in the darkness.

Pep, I whispered, look here, look this way.

I blocked it all out as a child, but it was all coming back to me now. This old painter was the reason I was too afraid to sleep, why I kept my television on all night and why I slept facing the wall with a pillow over my head.

Dreams of Palenque

As a boy, I traveled extensively throughout Mexico with my family. On one of these summer trips, driving through the dense jungles of Chiapas, we visited the ancient Mayan city of Palenque.

Even as a boy, Palenque felt familiar to me. I felt an organic connection to the place, to its history. I imagined its streets, then engulfed by jungle foliage and not fully excavated, crowded with the ghosts of those who had lived centuries before. I felt the power of Palenque and somehow knew that I belonged there, that Palenque was my home.

Memories of a past life.

It was as if I had been there many times before.

You had been.

Nowhere did I sense my ethereal link with Palenque more than in the Tomb of Pakal The Great, deep below the Temple of Inscriptions. Within this humid tomb of sweating stone, K'inich Janaab' Pakal, who ruled over Palenque for sixty-eight years and, who most certainly, had extraterrestrial links, was buried. Inside, his sarcophagus was sealed by a giant stone slab upon which was chronicled the great emperor's journey to Xibalba, the kingdom of death. At age 11, observing in awe the magnificence of this tomb, I was taken by a profound sense of déjà vu, a recognition that somehow, I had been here before.

Long before I ever travelled to Palenque, I dreamed of this royal burial chamber. The old painter would appear to me within the sweltering hollow of Pakal's Tomb. He would come, however, not as a painter but dressed in the ceremonial feathered robes and headdress of a Mayan high priest…

They were Quetzal feathers.

…chanting a prayer while smudging the tomb with a kind of strange incense. At his side, was a mammoth green jaguar, a living, breathing, growling statue, cut from jade and magically come to life.

The old painter, or high priest, greeted me with a ceremonial gesture; tapping his fist upon his forehead, pounding it hard upon his chest then, opening his hand, gesturing to the heavens. It was a kind of salute.

The sign of the Ghost Warrior.

This salute would later take on a profound meaning for me, upon my return from the Boulevard of the Dead, as a Ghost Warrior…

I gave you this name because you were one who died, walked among ghosts, and fought his own demons. As a Ghost Warrior, you would return to the Land of the Living, and fight to expose the evil forces inhibiting all of humanity from living out their divine plans.

… It would be a salute I would use with the players that I coached on the basketball court, to the students in my classroom and to my own children at home.

The fist to the forehead signifies that we are warriors of mind.

We are warriors of mind because we fight to learn.

The fist to the chest signifies that we are warriors of body.

We are warriors of body because we fight to keep our bodies strong by eating mindfully and exercising.

The hand outstretched to the heavens signifies that we are warriors of spirit.

We are warriors of spirit because we fight to keep alive the Seven Sacred Aspects…

Your Comanche Medicine Man's Seven Sacred Aspects…

…of respect, humility, compassion, truth, honesty, unconditional love and wisdom.

The teachings of a great man.

It was always the same dream. After saluting me, the old painter would offer me first a brush, the bristles of which appeared to be blue feathers. Quetzal feathers, I would assume…

Of course, but these particular feathers were different. They were blue.

Then, the old painter would offer me a bucket of blue paint.

"Paint the world blue," the old painter would instruct.

I had no idea what this old man meant by telling me this but, as a child, I was surprised when my father would also later direct me to paint the world blue.

That's why you were born. To paint the world blue.

But how did my father know?

An angel told him.

One night, when I was eight and having already visited Palenque many times in the dream world, my father and I were wrestling on his bed. He turned me over, tickled me a bit then told me, "you are going to grow up to be a great painter. You are going to paint the whole world blue."

I had never told my father or anyone about my dreams of Palenque, of the old Painter, the High Priest or the jade jaguar. So, how, I wondered, could my father have known to tell me …paint the world blue? Moreover, I had no idea at the time what either the old painter or my father meant by painting the world blue. I'm not sure to this day whether my father understood the significance of what he was saying, if he actually knew what the color blue was all about.

He knew intuitively. He listened to his own voice and that of his own guardian angel. The circle of angels is a small one. We all talk. He knew.

As for myself, I was too young and too scared to know.

"I don't want to be a painter!" I told the old painter, the mysterious High Priest, defiantly in my dreams. He would bow his head in sad defeat and then I'd wake up, sometimes to the menacing growls of a jaguar in my bedroom somewhere.

You were afraid, of course, but life would have been easier if you had listened.

We might have been able to avoid the Boulevard of the Dead altogether.

Maybe, but then we would have had no story to tell, no book to write.

While I told no one about my dreams, I did share with my mother that I thought my room was haunted. I told her of the shadows that would appear on my bedroom walls, the growling and of the voices that kept whispering out my name. Of course, she told me that there was nothing to fear, it was all my imagination, that there were no such things as voices in the dark or things that go bump in the night. She naturally attributed my nocturnal troubles to too much television and too many horror movies.

My father did believe, however, in the voices I was hearing and in the shadows I described. He was a different kind of guy who had experienced his own share of shadows on the wall, whispering voices and prophetic dreams. Sadly, after my parent's divorce, I saw my father only on weekends, so I didn't always have him there to reassure me, explain or validate the strange things I was seeing and hearing at night.

He was always there for you. It was you who avoided him.

I was my father's pride and joy, his boy, and he loved me more than anyone. Even more, I dare say, than my sister.

You were his boy.

I avoided my father, though, after a heart-wrenching divorce just as I avoided the old painter in my dreams. To some degree, there was the feeling, probably common among the children of divorce, that loving my father meant I didn't love my mother, who was constantly reminding me that my father didn't pay dime one for [me]. It became a choice of loyalty between my mother and my father. I chose my mom.

My father was an old man, his age a sign of his mortality and of my own. It scared me to think that he might die and thinking about his death drove me to thinking about my own eventual end. As I avoided everything that scared me, I avoided my own father. It was as a child, of course, that the various seeds of fear took root within me to rule over my life.

Fear is one of those things that keeps us from living out our dreams. That's the plan of the Man in Black and the purpose of his illusion.

Of this Man in Black and his illusion, we will learn more.

Rest assured.

As a child, I didn't want to hear voices or see shadows on my wall. I was afraid so I blocked out the old painter from my dreams, and the jade jaguar, too. I slept, cuddling up to my beloved basketball…

Henrietta, you named her. Your first love.

…with the lights and television on all night and made sure to face the wall when I lay in bed, afraid that I might see the shadows of the old painter and his feline familiar hovering at my bedside.

We were there every night, never giving up hope for you, whispering your name.

Road Trip

Now, in this strange alternate world, in my Civic, surfing through these swells of neon blue fog, I wasn't afraid of this old painter at all. It was like embarking on a road trip with an old buddy.

"Your death is a great opportunity," the old painter told me.

"My death?" I asked him.

"You went through a red."

"Yeah, I laughed, "that was close."

"More than close. You didn't make it, Pep."

Now shockingly it dawned on me where I was. The euphoric fog in my own head was beginning to clear somewhat but it was still like waking up from one dream and into another. Clearly, I was no longer driving with my wife down Main Street, into Loma, on our way to pick up a U-Haul so that we could make our move from the country back to the coast of Monterey Bay. Instead, I was now driving through some surreal blue fog, on some old street somewhere in nowhere land.

"On this boulevard you have a chance," he responded.

"to realize your highest potential and fulfill your life's purpose."

"What does it matter if I'm dead?" I begged.

"It matters, Pep."

Outside, I now saw the indistinct silhouettes of dozens of people, sluggishly making their way through the blue gloom.

"Those people, they're dead, too?"

The old painter nodded.

Watching these specters shuffle aimlessly through the fog filled me with an overwhelming feeling of hopelessness. Somehow, I felt deeply connected to their sadness, as if their pain was my own.

"What is this place?" I asked.

"The Boulevard of the Dead," the old painter said with a wry smile.

"This isn't Heaven?"

"It's on the way. We're sort of on the outskirts of Heaven."

I thought about my wife and our baby on the way and asked if they were alright.

"I'm your angel, Pep," the old painter shrugged, "I'm here for you!

I still am.

"My angel?" I asked, "my guardian angel?"

The old painter nodded.

"You're here to guide me to the light?" I asked.

To enlightenment.

You didn't answer, only flashing a coy smile.

"We're going to drive through this fog until we hit Heaven?" I asked, anxiously seeking out answers.

"No."

We had a few stops to make first. Besides, we couldn't go to Heaven on an empty stomach.

The old painter laughed. It was a deep, bellowing, full-hearted, joyous laugh. Again, I recognized that laugh. It was my father's hearty laugh, but this old painter was not my father.

THE PANADERIA MEXICANA

I was delighted to breathe in the aroma of freshly baked breads coming in through the air vents of my car.

"How about some pan dulce and a nice hot cup of champurado?" the old painter asked, pointing up the street to a dingy little bakery called "Panaderia Mexicana," its splintered sign hanging on a slant by one rusted nail over the entrance.

We parked along the curb in front of the panaderia. The smell of bolillos and pastries saturated the foggy air.

A little bell jingled as we walked into the bakery.

It was worth it just to walk in and sniff.

"Are you sure we're not in Heaven?" I joked, blissfully buzzed by the wonderful aroma.

The Altar

Heaven, indeed, one seemingly made just for me. On the walls, I saw posters of all my boyhood heroes; of Zapata, the Mexican rebel who fought for "Tierra y Libertad," of Muhammad Ali, the "greatest" boxer of all time, Sean Connery, still the only James Bond, Charles Bronson, "The Mechanic," and Clint Eastwood as "Dirty Harry."

There was another poster on the wall behind the pantry, hung over the swinging doors that led to a kitchen. It was a framed 1931 billboard of "Ravel's Bolero" at the Hollywood Bowl, featuring my father, one of the great Flamenco dancers of all time.

The highlight of the store was a beautifully decorated altar set up in honor of Dia De Los Muertos, or Day of the Dead, a Latin holiday celebrating the lives of those who have passed on. This altar, adorned by cempasuchil and colorful crepe paper flowers, was similar to those my mother still sets up every October with candles, sugar skulls, a calavera display – in this case, skeletons dressed up as mariachis - and a few loaves of pan de muerto, a delicious variety of sweetened bread flavored with anise, some orange peel and topped with red sugar to simulate blood over bones.

Most important, on this altar, was a display of photographs and mementos honoring the recently, and not so recently, departed. There was a brand-new leather Wilson basketball mounted on the altar, "Henrietta" scrawled along its worn leather surface in black marker. There was a pair of ebony castanets crafted by my father, my father's cap, a soup bowl, a picture of my uncle and, pinned to the wall, my own driver's license.

There was something else also, something I didn't recognize from anywhere in my life. A fluffy blue feather was laid beside my father's castanets.

The pantry was loaded up with pan dulces and Mexican candies; jamoncillos, sugared calabasas and other fruits and vegetables. A hot pot of champurado, a rich chocolaty drink, was simmering behind the counter. I was so overwhelmed by the selection of treats that I just couldn't make up my mind as to what to choose.

"Choose it all," the old painter teased.

You could have eaten as much as you wanted, it's not like you were counting calories!

A Little Boy Living in His Head

I turned to see a little boy by the window. He sat by himself, wearing a red striped shirt, coloring and drawing. His head was bald but for a little black sprout of hair just above his forehead. I was saddened to see this little boy, so alone, so detached, so immersed in his drawing. After a moment, I recognized this sad boy. He was me.

"A sad little boy," the old painter observed, "living his life in his head."

Living in my head would be a running theme in my life. Before the Boulevard of the Dead, it was a quality I was ashamed of but, after I returned to the Land of the Living, it was something I would fight for.

"You're living in your head, Pep." Jake would often tell me.

"Always walking around with your head in the clouds," my wife would snip, snapping her fingers ghetto-style and rolling her eyes in disgust.

On the Boulevard of the Dead, I saw where it all began, the origins of my retreat from the real world into my head. While my sister, who I don't think heard any voices, nor saw old painters or jade jaguars, escaped the tumult of our childhood by diving into the world, embracing people, fighting for control and material success, seeking out attention and making sure she was always the star, I sought out invisibility, retreating into my imaginary world.

Seeing myself in the panaderia brought back some sad memories of early childhood; my mother and father fighting late into the night while my sister and I pretended to sleep, of a painful divorce, of voices that spoke to me from the shadows, of a jaguar's growl. Even then, at eight-years-old, I found escape in my head, in my imagination, in the stories I told myself to put myself to sleep at night and the pictures I would draw, and by immersing myself in television. Then, as now, I never slept. Hardly a night went by that I didn't wake up at one in the morning from nightmares, maybe dreaming that my father was dead, or of the old painter chanting prayers within the Tomb of Pakal and beckoning me to join him.

I dreamed of my father dying often. He was sixty when I was born, my mother much, much younger. In his prime, my father was an internationally famous dancer, a pioneer in the art of flamenco. He danced to fame, surfing that first wave of the original Latin Explosion in the early part of the last century. Although, he smoked and drank heavily, dancing and a romantic playful spirit made him a spectacular physical specimen well into his late seventies. If not for a devastating hit and run that crippled and aged him, it seemed at the time that my father might have lived forever.

I remember my father crying out often to my mother, always late at night, "I'm old! I'm old! You're going to leave me so that I die alone!" Thus, the inevitability of death was introduced to me and it scared me. I was horribly disturbed by the thought of his death, his mortality, the idea of watching him wither away, losing my daddy. That thought and the recognition of my own temporality, petrified me.

My father's snoring rocked the house. It was loud and thunderous. Still, I was strangely comforted by the sound of his snores because that snoring affirmed for me that he was still breathing and that he was still alive.

Often, I crawled out of my bed in the middle of the night, my sister sleeping soundly in the bed next to mine, seeking shelter from the nightmares, voices and other night sounds, in my parent's bedroom.

There I found my spot at the foot of their bed to watch all-night movies on their black and white television while my father snored.

After my parent's divorce, as my friends spent the daylight hours playing outside, I locked myself in my bedroom, curtains closed, the television on, drawing pictures of my favorite television stars and super heroes. Drawing always came easy to me as I was blessed, without ever taking a lesson, with the capacity to illustrate whatever I saw around me or whatever I imagined. Marvel Comics inspired most of my artwork and I spent hours drawing my favorite super heroes. For me, the outside world was so unstable and scary that I naturally created my own world in my bedroom, a world I felt I could control in my head. In my head, I felt safe. In my head I lived much of my life.

You still do.

Yes, but proudly now.

On the wall, behind the boy in the panaderia, I saw rise the menacing dark shadow of a jaguar. The boy ignored it, focusing his attention on a picture he was drawing. It was a picture of Thor, his favorite Marvel superhero. As the old painter had observed, the boy lived in his head, lost in his own world, a movie playing in his brain. With each mark of a crayon, the boy made an urgent whooshing sound as if the wind was blowing hard, then hummed a movie score to accompany and enhance whatever drama he was drawing on paper. Sometimes, as he shaded in his drawings, he hummed or whistled the theme from an old Universal horror, like *The Wolfman* or *The Bride of Frankenstein* - just to heighten the mood of the world he was drawing.

Every now and then the little boy would look up and gaze through the window into the blue fog and at the specters outside.

"His whole life is coming undone," I said of myself.

He was afraid of the world outside his own head.

I wanted to comfort this boy, whose parents were divorcing, to console myself, but my attention was suddenly diverted by the sound of heavy footsteps behind me. I turned to see a large man emerge from the kitchen. The baker. His hands and face were caked in flour and dry dough.

"What can I get you?" the baker asked, overly anxious to serve me.

The sight of this baker sent an instant chill up my spine. Though his pock-marked features were obscured, I still recognized him somehow, maybe his voice or his eyes, through the mask of dried flour that covered his face.

"I know him," I whispered to the old painter.

"You know everyone here," the old painter whispered back.

"The man I'm thinking of is dead. I heard that he died of lymphoma."

"Only dead people walk this boulevard."

The Bully

Chris Driscoll was the massive, pock-marked bully who harassed me throughout my high school years. Along with his racist pals, he humiliated me with racial slurs, taunted me and beat me up regularly. One of the very few Latino kids in an all white school, I was an easy target.

My mother was a beautiful and well to do girl of Hungarian-Jewish origins from New York, with a PhD in Mexican Folklore and a passion for Ranchera music. My stepfather, Horace, was a brilliant German with a PhD in Spanish literature, a fine writer and a good ear for music. Together, they would later travel throughout Mexico as a popular Ranchera singing duet. To this day, they still sing all over Mexico and Los Angeles. My real father was a Mexican Catholic who told everyone he was from Spain.

So, I grew up a white, Hungarian Mexican American Catholic Jewish boy in Los Angeles. I was of such an eclectic blend that I would often joke, "I don't know whether to say 'Oy' or 'Aye." I wasn't brown, I wasn't white. I was just me, a person without a label. In Mexico, our friends called me a Gringo, in America I was a Beaner.

To Chris and his ignorant crew, I was just a spic or a wetback. This was the crowd that joked about ten Mexicans in a Chevy or four families in a garage. These were the guys that pushed me around just because I was brown.

I took it all with a smile, of course, laughed at all their put downs and behaved the fool they made me out to be. What else could I do? I was all alone and, other than my sister, I was one of the very few minorities at my school. While I was able to fake it pretty well to the outside world, while I may have appeared laid back, care-free and confident, my smile masked a raging self-loathing that manifested itself in later years with reckless behavior and self-destruction.

I hated high school and Chris Driscoll accounted for much of the why. If not for the escape I found in film, comic books, basketball, and James Bond; if not for the sanctuary of my bedroom and the world of my imagination, if I didn't have my head to live in and escape into, I never would have survived those hellish high school years. Prejudice and hatred exist everywhere but, in my own high school experience, Chris Driscoll engineered much of the hatred towards me.

The Long Green Line

One morning, I arrived at school to find that everyone seemed to be staring at me, whispering behind my back or laughing. At first, I thought it was all my imagination, that I was just being paranoid. But, as I walked through the crowded corridor to my locker, the chatter seemed to build, and I noticed a spray-painted green line on a wall.

Freshly painted, the green line extended all the way down the corridor and around a corner. Approaching my locker, a flock of students crowded around me, laughing and taunting. The green line became an arrow that pointed directly to my locker, "SPIC" written above it. The laughter reverberated around me and, humiliated, I spotted Chris Driscoll at the top of a staircase, smirking and flipping me the bird.

The School Bus

A few weeks later, I climbed onto a school bus after school. The last one on the bus, I was exhausted from basketball practice and my arms were loaded with books and dirty gym clothes. Inside, I saw Kathy at the very back of the bus. She was a cheerleader and my high school dream girl. Of course, I was much too shy to ever approach her on my own but on this particular day, she actually waved at me and gestured for me to join her at the back of the bus. Nervous and sweating, I thought that maybe this was the chance I was waiting for and I somehow mustered the courage just to return her wave and mouth, "Hi."

I started towards her, making my shy and clumsy way through the crowded aisle, stepping over outstretched feet trying to trip me up, dodging sharp elbows and jabbing hands trying to push me to the floor. Then, Chris popped up from one of the seats, four buddies rising with him.

"Where you going, spic?" Chris taunted, smashing his chest into mine, pushing me back. I tried to back down, but other kids shoved me forward.

"Leave him alone," I remember someone screaming. There were some other compassionate voices but mostly a chorus of jeers from a bored mob hungry to see something they could talk about in the morning. Not even the driver tried to stop it. He just watched, giving his approval with a thumbs up to the boys.

"Stay away from the white girls," I heard the driver say. Hard to believe but true.

Then, they were hard upon me. Chris grabbed me by the ear, someone else took my hair and I was dragged through the aisle, my books and gym clothes spilling out everywhere, and tossed out of the bus. Falling hard on the concrete, the back of my head hitting the sidewalk, I was nearly knocked out. Honestly, I don't know what kept me conscious, it was such a hard blow. It's difficult today to recall completely all that came afterwards. I was so stunned, so dazed, my body went numb to the pain. I don't even remember feeling the brutal attack that followed, the nasty punches to my head, the sharp kicks to my side and, finally, my notebooks slammed against my face to end it all.

Even then, beaten, bruised and dazed, my underwear slung about my head, humiliated before my big crush, I still tried to fake a smile, like I was in on the joke. Inside the bus, I saw Chris, yet again, laughing and flipping me the bird. The bus driver smirked, closed the doors and drove away.

Chris was the unrelenting engineer behind my systematic humiliation. Rather than tell my mother or go to a school official (which I chose not to do), I did nothing. To do something, I felt, would have made my situation even worse. I was too humiliated. As with everything else in my life, fear dominated, and I felt powerless to stop him.

I hated Chris Driscoll, I hated him almost as much as I was now learning to hate myself. Sadly, I was beginning to believe that I was as stupid and worthless as he and his cohorts told me I was. I hated him. I can't count the many nights I put myself to sleep imagining that I was beating the hell out of him or, I'm embarrassed to admit, wishing him dead. How ironic, I thought, that he was here now, dead, on this haunted boulevard.

"What can I get you?" Chris repeated. Seeing him again brought back all the pain of high school disgrace, all the unresolved fury. Trembling, I clenched my fist.

"Two pan dulces and two hot cups of your delicious champurado," the old painter stepped in to say.

Chris smiled politely at the old painter.

"Alright," he said, pouring the old painter a steaming hot cup of champurado.

Chris then leaned across the counter and offered me a plate of pan dulce and hot champurado. I refused it. I wanted nothing from him. All I wanted to do was hit him, hurt him like he hurt me. He saw my hands balling up, ready to throw down.

"Hit me if you like," Chris said, straightening up and closing his eyes, bracing himself for the blow, "You need to. I deserve it. Hit me."

I was taken aback momentarily by his offer, surprised. Here was my chance. The chance I dreamed of throughout high school, my chance to get even and hurt Chris Driscoll, to make him feel and truly understand my pain. I clenched my fist tighter and drew it back, ready to let it fly, to break his face wide open.

"Hit me," he said again, waiting for the inevitable.

I hesitated before throwing down, wondering for a moment whether this was a joke or not, looking quickly around to see that I wasn't being set up, making sure that his buddies weren't lurking somewhere in the panaderia, waiting to jump me.

"Hit him," the old painter encouraged me.

Then, Chris began to cry, tears streaming down his face, soaking the dry mask of dough and washing it partially away so that I could see his pock-marked baby face, looking as if he hadn't aged a bit since high school.

"Hit me!" he demanded, he pleaded, his face veiled by a torrent of tears.

Chris the bully was no longer there. It was a different person who stood before me now. One who suddenly seemed so humbled, so defeated, so vulnerable. This was not the same mean-spirited kid who tormented me in school. Here was a broken soul.

Life does that. It humbles us all.

I couldn't hit him.

You were also a different man.

I dropped my fist.

"You humiliated me," I told Chris.

"I'm sorry," he sobbed, "I am ashamed. I'll do anything to make things right."

He fought his own demons, Pep, and had his own journey to redemption before being allowed to enter the light.

In his remorse...

And, in your willingness to forgive...

...I felt a warm rush overtake me and it seemed that a piece of me had returned to me.

Like some long lost and traumatized bit of your soul had been found and restored.

Yes.

You let go of the hate that had kept a fragment of your soul locked up in that panaderia where he was waiting for you.

"So," Chris asked desperately, offering me the plate of pan and champurado again, "Is it right, are we okay?"

Now, so suddenly disarmed, I nodded, taking the plate and the cup of champurado.

"Thank you," he said, relieved, circling the counter to embrace me. How ironic was this? Chris Driscoll hugging me somewhere on the road to Heaven, in a panaderia. He pulled off his apron and tossed it behind the counter.

"Great!" Chris said jubilantly, rubbing flour from his hands and checking his wrist-watch, "I have to go."

Chris reached quickly behind the counter and snagged a loaf of pan de muerto from the altar.

One for the road.

Chris paused momentarily to look upon the little boy. We turned to see him, lost in his drawing of Thor, the boy was making thunder and lightning sounds.

"Is he okay?" Chris asked the old painter, truly concerned.

"I think so," the old painter responded, "This is a very good start."

Bells jingled, and we turned back to find the door swung open. Chris had taken off. Sipping champurado, my whole being warmed by its magical chocolaty blend, I stepped forward to peer out the window where I could see Chris making his way up the boulevard, dodging the specters that crowded the fog-soaked street, cutting resolutely through the thick blue mist, munching on pan de muerto. Unlike the others who shuffled mindless and zombie-like along the Boulevard of the Dead, Chris seemed to know exactly where he was going.

As Chris spirited through the fog, I noticed that at least three or four of the shadowy figures he passed just disappeared. As they vanished, more waves of wonderful warm energy passed through me. I watched Chris until he also just disappeared within the heavy blue fog that crushed in upon the boulevard.

Watching Chris make his way to Heaven, I felt relieved of a great weight, exorcized of so many demons. Real or imagined, there was a miracle in that moment.

"One less lost and broken soul on this Boulevard of the Dead," the old painter observed.

"He looks happy," I said, my eyes searching through the fog for any sign of Chris.

"Not Chris," the old painter said, pointing out the window to another shadowy figure in the fog, "you!"

A teenage boy in a letterman's jacket emerged from the fog and looked at us through the window, so close that his breath misted the glass. His face was illuminated by the dull orange glow of a corner street lamp. I recognized instantly another version of myself. It was me at seventeen, the me so traumatized by Chris. We smiled at each other through the glass. Then, the teenage boy disappeared and, again, I felt a magical rush of warm energy surge through me.

"What is that warm rush?" I asked.

"That is you coming back together again," the old painter explained, breaking off a piece of pan dulce, dipping it in champurado and sticking it in his mouth, "hopefully, we have enough time to bring most of *you* back together again."

It suddenly occurred to me that all the specters staggering through the whirling blue mist, every single one of them, not just a few, were incarnations of myself, me at distinct stages of my life. I recognized me everywhere.

"Everyone is me!" I gasped, the realization hitting me hard.

Everyone is you. And you are everyone.

At some point, while we were still in the panaderia, the old painter and I sat at a dining booth by a window, across from the little boy. At the center of our table a white candle burned.

No Light in a Dead Man's Eyes

"Pep," the old painter asked, wolfing down a piece of pan dulce, "have you ever looked into a dead man's eyes?"

It seemed like a random question at the time.

The question was strictly rhetorical. I wasn't expecting an answer.

No. I had never looked into a dead man's eyes.

"No light in a dead man's eyes," the old painter spoke in a soft voice.

No light in a dead man's eyes?

Days after my return to the Land of the Living, recovering in Loma Community Hospital, I grappled with the meaning of that seemingly random comment.

It's all about the light.

Broken all over, my organs swollen by trauma, a chest tube inserted between my ruptured ribs to suck out the pus and infection that flooded my chest cavity, my eventual rehabilitation would be a horribly painful ordeal, but it allowed for plenty of time for me...

For us...

...to reflect on the meaning of my life and... my death.

We had some great conversations in that hospital room and throughout your rehab.

There was no grace in the way I would deal with my mortality when I returned to life, no poise in the manner I would handle the possibility that I might not make it, no bravery in my approach to pain. I cried every day, sometimes because of the pain itself, and sometimes out of sheer gratitude for being alive. Many times I cried because I couldn't reconcile my feelings with what sometimes, even then, seemed the random nature of life and death.

There is nothing random about life and death.

My broken rib punctured my left lung and grazed my heart.

"If your rib had gone even a half couple centimeters deeper into your heart," my surgeon explained, "you would have been gone."

A couple centimeters? If the rib went that far, why didn't it go further? Surely the force of the crash was enough to impale my heart as well. Why didn't it? Obsessing on that couple of centimeters brought me to tears throughout the early days of my rehab, when I was still unconvinced as to the *reality* of my trip to the other side, when there was still a question in my mind as to whether or not I would survive at all. For, despite my ethereal tour through the Boulevard of the Dead, I was still very much afraid.

Friends, who doubted my eventual near-death claims...

There will always be those who doubt.

...have argued that my little peek into the other side should have filled me with hope and a greater determination to fight my way back to health.

Nonsense. It took a long while before you were able to grasp or come to terms with the full meaning of your experience.

Obviously, my odyssey through the Boulevard of the Dead was not yet enough to quell my immediate fears, doubts, tears or my physical pain. It was still more a dream than a memory. The validation that my experience was real, and not simply a dream, would come only after the daily discourses with my guardian angel that followed my return to the Land of the Living.

Those discourses continue, as you can see, to this day.

It would take several years of dialogues with my guardian angel before I was truly able to comprehend, make sense, and have faith in the truth and significance of my near-death experience. That wisdom and faith would come with my decision to finally believe in myself, to have faith in my own voice, a voice which I would finally hear upon a bridge just outside the Boulevard of the Dead.

We will come to that.

Since my accident, the old painter has visited me many times.

We are in constant communication.

He is my guardian angel.

I am.

Unlike the days of my childhood, when I denied him, I now welcome his visits and enjoy our epic discourses.

As do I.

I didn't understand what the old painter was getting at in that panaderia. It is only through our long deliberations since then that I now know what he meant when he offered to me in a hushed tone this insight; No light in a dead man's eyes.

It's all about the light. It is the why; the why we are and the what we are. It is in the light that we decide the lives we will live. It is to the light that we return when our lives are done before embarking on another one. It is the spark that resides in and animates our bodies – those most sacred temples which house the light of our souls. It is that very light that the material world, ruled by the Man in Black...

Ah, yes, him again...

...works to block, douse and divide.

We must fight to know the light.

We will come to see that this Man in Black keeps humanity enslaved in deceitful darkness, blocking our connection with the light-sonic God-force frequency we have referred to as...

...The Quetzal.

Again, it is the Quetzal which connects us all with our creator and within its light that we realize our oneness with all of humanity.

What the old painter was trying to tell me in a morbid way, as we polished off our pan dulce in the panaderia was that light is not reflected off the eyes but instead emitted from the eyes, from within us all, from within our very temples. That light, I now know, is perfection, that light is divine, that light is who we are, it is God.

That light is the Quetzal.

We are all light. We are all connected in that same light. We are all one.

We are one.

Respect, of course, was the first of the Medicine Man's Seven Sacred Aspects, those timeless virtues we should all be working to incorporate into our lives.

Respect for all life, for all people and for ourselves, is achieved through faith in that light, with the realization that the light shining in our eyes is the same light that shines in the eyes of all men and all living things.

Thus, Chris and I learned of our oneness. We were always one. ***It seems a cliché by now but nevertheless a truth; Hurting others serves only to hurt ourselves and, in loving others, we love ourselves.***

In this same way, everyone is me and I am everyone. I AM. ***We all ARE.***

OLD PAINTER'S GALLERY 2

The Divine Plan

We choose the lives we live in the spirit world. In Heaven, we decide our mission and our purpose, we compose with God our Divine Plan and we are sometimes shown how our mission in life fits with God's overall vision for the universe. We choose our circumstance, we choose our families, the people that come into our lives. It is all quite awesome.

Our dreams are our purpose. Our dreams are God's way of slipping through the radar defenses of the illusion – and the trappings of life, we will soon learn, is a malevolent illusion – reminding us of our purpose in life.

It is God's will that our dreams come true. But, that doesn't mean that we all live out our dreams. Just because the Divine Plan is in place doesn't guarantee we realize our destinies. Our own free will, more often than not, prevents many of us from accomplishing our missions – whether from fear, guilt, lack of preparation, most of us do not live in true fulfillment because we do not live out our dreams.

There is nobody to blame for our dreams not being realized. Not those who stood in our way, not the many obstacles which sprang up before us and certainly not God who assigned us our dreams in the first place. We have only ourselves to blame. We chose this divine plan, we chose those people, those obstacles and the lessons to be learned before our present lives – and we do live many lives – began, in the spirit world. There is no one to blame but ourselves. We chose our lives. We are accountable for the lives we live or the lives we don't live -more accountable than we ever imagined.

Still, there may also be another, independent and more sinister, will at play here when it comes to obstructing our divine plans. As we will see, this insidious entity is the prime architect of the illusion which keeps many of us from realizing our dreams.

The Divine Plan, the stage by stage road map leading to our purpose and the realization of our dreams, can, if we listen to our own divinely inspired voices, perceive and obey the divine signs around us, be relatively easy or, depending on the choices we make, much more difficult when we fall off the path. Still, it is never too late. The universe always offers us a way and the means to get back on track, although these off-road journeys may be extremely challenging and taxing.

Never forget, we all have a purpose in life and that purpose is our dreams. Your passion is your purpose. God wants our dreams to come true. It is God's will. But God won't do it for us. There are no push button solutions to life. We are indeed responsible for our own healing. We are accountable to our dreams. Never give up on your dreams, whatever the hardship, keep fighting and never surrender. We are all meant to live our dreams.

THE FOG

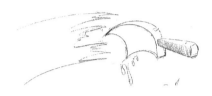

I found myself back in the car, with the old painter...

Of course...

...cruising again down the Boulevard of the Dead. The fog was thick now and it had lost its neon blue glow. This was a dark gray fog, almost black, packing down upon us. My high-beams were powerless to pierce through this murky gloom and, unable to see anything through it, I lifted my foot from the gas pedal and slowed my Honda to a stop.

"Why are you stopping?" the old painter asked, sorting through several paint brushes laid out carefully upon his lap. They were strange looking brushes, their uneven bluish bristles looking more like the tail feathers of a bird.

As in your dreams of Palenque, they were the tail feathers of the Quetzal.

"I can't see," I answered, "there's too much fog."

"Too much fog?" the old painter laughed, "I can see perfectly well the light at the end of this road."

I looked hard into the fog, my windshield wipers on high, but couldn't see any light at all. I couldn't even see the road.

"What light?" I asked.

This fog was of your own making. It represented all the lies and worldly addictions that you were clinging to, blocking you from seeing your own light, keeping you from knowing your own divine origin, your divine plan, your purpose, your dream. We all need to commune with that light, have faith in that light that burns within us all and live the light that we are. We must liberate ourselves from the lies that fog over our connection with this Quetzal for, as you know, only in the Quetzal, in that light, can we know God.

The question is, how? How do we live in this light?

There is a way. The Ghost Warrior Way. Meditation, nutrition, exercise.

Since my recovery, the old painter would teach me more and more about light, the Quetzal, dreams, the Man in Black and his lies.

More than twenty years' worth of running dialogue, meditations and life lessons.

For that moment, my attention was fixed on the assortment of paint brushes that the old painter laid across his lap.

"How much of your life," the old painter asked me, organizing his brushes from biggest to smallest on his lap, "have you lived in this dark fog?"

How much of your life had been a lie?

I didn't know how to answer.

"Pep," he continued with an exasperated sigh, "Did you live out your dreams?"

I shrugged.

"Yes or no?"

"I was a teacher," I responded defensively, "I worked with kids. I coached basketball."

That was not a yes.

It was sort of a yes. Since the days of the *White Shadow*, a '70's television series about a white basketball coach working at an inner city high school, I dreamed about being a teacher and a varsity basketball coach. Like the lead character, Coach Ken Reeves, played by the late Ken Howard, I wanted to work in a tough and disadvantaged school somewhere, save at-risk kids, overcome all the odds and win basketball championships.

But for a brief detour down the Boulevard of the Dead, I would grow up, teach and coach at various disadvantaged schools over the course of a 30-year career, work with at-risk youth and win a few league championships…

The most recent championship, of course, alongside your son, Dylan, as your starting point guard.

Would it be simple coincidence or destiny that I would someday enjoy my greatest success as a basketball coach at the very high school in which the *White Shadow* was actually filmed?

No more a coincidence than blue being the primary color of that school. Everything has meaning.

At the time of my death all those years ago, my dreams of being a teacher and a basketball coach had been accomplished. Still, if that had really been the end, there would have been so much of my life left unfulfilled.

There was so much more that you were supposed to do.

"You were a great teacher!" The old painter responded.

"That was my dream."

"But, you had other dreams."

"Yes, I did."

Dreams that you ran away from.

I wanted to write and heal people with my stories.

You are living out your dreams right now through your teaching, your coaching and...by writing this book.

I am.

"You ran away from those dreams?" the old painter continued, still sorting out his brushes, "of writing and telling stories. Why?"

"I don't know."

"You don't know? What was it the Medicine Man taught us about 'I don't know?'

The Medicine Man? Was he here? I was very excited at the possibility that I might meet this Medicine Man in shades on the Boulevard of the Dead. I never really knew him. He wasn't a friend of mine. I was but one of 300 people who sat in the main ballroom of a Ramada Inn at one of his many workshops on Traditional Indian Medicine. Still, his impact on my life (and on others) was such that I felt like I knew him well. As with Jake, to whom the Medicine Man appeared many times in dreams, he would usually appear in my own dreams, wearing his signature shades, at crucial times in my life to deliver important messages.

It had been nearly ten years since I attended his Traditional Indian Medicine seminars with Jake and, while there were rumors about his demise, I didn't know for sure whether the Medicine Man was alive or dead.

The Medicine Man taught us that you are the only one who knows what's going on with you. Nobody else can know. When someone says they don't know, what they really mean is …

…They don't want to know.

Time on Earth is sacred. It is not something we can afford to waste. No time to waste on not knowing.

"What is it you don't want to know?" the old painter asked.

You were blessed with so many talents. So many brushes. You could draw anything you saw exactly as you saw it, you were a fine athlete, you were a wonderful storyteller.

"I was afraid that I wasn't good enough," I replied, "to share my gifts."

"But, you were!"

You never left the classroom or stopped coaching basketball.

My safe place.

Like hiding in your bedroom, living in your head, drawing with the television on. Like hiding in the dark corner of the La Reina movie theater watching Bond flicks by yourself.

I figured that's where I was meant to be. That I was a classroom teacher and a basketball coach. My dreams of writing books, storytelling and even of making movies were wrong.

Dreams are never wrong. They guide us to our purpose. Divine mandates, written into our divine plans. How can that be wrong? What is that old saying? Our passion is our purpose.

I didn't know that then. I was afraid of failure and of…

…the accountability attached should your dreams actually be realized?

Possibly.

I also didn't feel I deserved my dreams to come true, that I somehow wasn't worthy.

A feeling that also haunted your father.

True. But, also, I felt that I didn't deserve success. I didn't work hard for my talents. They just came…

…too easily?

Yes. I believed that success in anything could only come through hard work and I never had to work for my talents. They were just there.

If anyone complimented me on any of my artistic skills, I would most often respond with a no, I'm not that good rather than thank you. It was almost as if I was apologizing for being good. As I never trained or worked hard for these gifts, I simply denied them. I felt like I was faking my talents. That I was a liar.

It was easier to simply believe that your sole purpose was to save kids in the classroom and through basketball.

Yes.

Never dreaming that your classroom or the lessons of your gymnasium might extend beyond the bounds of the four walls that enclosed you? No idea that your classroom could be so much larger?

I didn't see that then, of course. My death would change my entire perspective on my life. At that time, however, I used basketball and whatever my assigned classroom curriculum was as tools to save kids.

Save them from what?

From believing in the lies, I guess and from quitting. I wanted to inspire them to pursue their dreams and never to quit on them."

You already knew about the lie, then?

I must have. I sensed, somehow, that reality; its expectations and standards, was a lie. I didn't want kids to assimilate and believe in that lie.

I wanted to help kids believe in themselves, to have more faith in their own voices than in the voices of others. I wanted them all to live out their dreams. I didn't want them to give up on their dreams or get sidetracked from the purpose in their lives.

As you did? As you were sidetracked? As you allowed the "rational" voices of all those who bought into the lie drown out your own voice? My voice?

Yes.

Not knowing that those lies were the work of the Man in Black.

Not knowing.

But, now you know.

Now, I know.

"Pep," the old painter laid his hand on my shoulder, "you were good enough, you are good enough, your dreams were right, they are right."

By fulfilling our own dreams, we inspire others to also remember God's will in their own lives and thus bring all people closer to God.

"We are all meant to make it," the old painter continued with a smile, "That is God's Will."

I know.

We are all meant to live out all of our dreams...

Unless, of course, we don't.

Exactly. Because of the decisions we make and the time that we waste.

Then we end up on our own Boulevard of the Dead feeling strangely unfulfilled with the lives that we lived.

Just because we have a divine plan doesn't mean we will live those plans out.

Free will?

Free will within the context of a lie. How can we make good use of free will when we are all brain washed by a malevolent illusion that provides us with the database by which we make our decisions?

We can't.

How better to expose this evil illusion than by living out our dreams?

A revolution against a false reality?

It will take warriors. Revolutions have been fought before, against governments and tyranny. But the warriors who fought and led these campaigns did so within the context of the illusion. These past revolutions were only diversions to keep our focus away from the illusion itself – where the fight should really be directed.

Living out our dreams is part of this fight. Remembering our purpose is the beginning, doing what we are meant to do, connecting with God, revealing the truth.

Before the Boulevard of the Dead, I wasted a lot of time.

You did. You don't now, do you?

Not a minute.

Your classroom is so much bigger than you can imagine, your lessons so much more important than the curriculum you are paid to teach. Maybe, it all starts with this book about our journey through the Boulevard of the Dead.

Maybe.

The old painter popped open a can of paint by his feet and began to mix it with a stick he pulled out from one of his many pockets. It was a broken tree branch.

"My God-stick," the old painter remarked with another of his knowing smiles as he mixed the blue paint.

Many years later, on a cliff overlooking the Ojai Valley, on that day blanketed by a mystical pink mist, my four-year-old son, Dylan, would pick up a broken branch off the nature trail and call it his God-stick. Through this stick, he said, God spoke to him.

Mixing paint, the old painter continued, "God gave us the power to overcome the lies of the Man in Black."

"The Man in Black?"

The liar, the fallen angel, the master of illusions and stealer of souls. Known by many names, he is Satan.

The old painter chuckled as he continued to stir, "Your dreams of writing, making movies and telling stories were meant to be realized. Your teaching and coaching is all a part of the same dream. These are your passions. They are the brushes with which you paint the world blue."

The old painter dipped one of his many feathered brushes into the paint. Again, If I was really dead and done with, if I had not come back, it would have been an incomplete life somehow, a life unfulfilled; a life having not realized my full potential.

That is, sadly, how life ends for so many – un-fulfillment.

Our talents are Divine blessings. They come easily and with no effort, talents we never trained or worked for.

As I said, I never truly believed in my talents. I didn't feel they were real. Those talents came too easily.

They are God's gifts to you. That should have been all the validation you needed to believe in. For you, Pep, those talents were nothing you had to work for or earn, just mysterious gifts you were supposed to be grateful for, humbled by and develop.

But, I didn't believe.

No, not then but now...

Now, I know that those gifts were among the tools I was blessed with to fulfill my purpose in life.

Brushes by which to paint the world blue.

You had been running away from your purpose since you were a child, hiding from your dreams. Just as you found refuge from me and the pain of your childhood in your bedroom, drawing and watching television, on the basketball court and in the gym, you sought similar escape in your classroom, running away from an even higher purpose and the full responsibility of your divine plan.

You weren't fulfilled at the time of your death because you didn't completely fulfill the directives of your mission on Earth. The directives you assigned yourself in the spirit world. It was God's will that you inspire others to pursue their dreams so that they do not succumb to the same fears (born of the Devil's lies) that disconnected you from the Quetzal and held you back. It was not God's will that you sacrifice some of your own dreams while you live out others. You, all of us, were meant to have it all.

The old painter offered me a paint-soaked brush.

"I tell you, again," the old painter said with a reassuring smile, "As I would tell my own children, all those I love and even myself, you were meant for greater things."

"Oh, yeah," I answered, smugly, "And what would those greater things be?"

"Maybe you should have written a book," he responded with another chuckle, pointing at the bag on my lap and at the cans of paint by his own feet, "You have many passions, many talents. You were blessed with all the brushes you needed to execute God's will and live out your true purpose here on Earth."

"Which was?"

"To paint the world blue."

I took the brush from the old painter's hand. He sighed with great relief.

"Finally. I offered you this brush many times before in your dreams," the old painter said with a satisfied grin, "I told you to paint the world blue. You blocked out my voice. Maybe here on this Boulevard of the Dead you can finally figure it all out."

I looked up and was surprised to see that the old painter was no longer beside me.

I was there.

The passenger seat was empty, and the car door opened. Outside, the fog lifted just a bit and I could see that I had somehow, despite the thick black fog that obstructed my view, parked perfectly alongside the curb in front of a dilapidated little barber shop called, "Dona Julia's Peluqueria."

OLD PAINTER'S GALLERY 3

The Illusion

Living within the Quetzal as I do, I have received little glimpses here and there of the truth outside the projection most of us accept as reality.

It is enough to say that nothing that we see here is real. Everything is an illusion, a projection engineered by the Man in Black, Lucifer. All designed to harvest our souls, the light within us, for eternity. We are all slaves within an elaborate interactive game, a Truman Show, a Matrix, which we have been programmed to accept as reality. This projection is supported by various mechanisms of deception

If you can imagine the Quetzal, God's divine frequency, as a computer software that has been hacked and compromised by a malevolent virus, created by the Man in Black's ingenious dark minions of deception, then you might begin to see the precarious situation we are all in.

This illusion is, of course, an external projection – as one would see on a movie screen. This external projection emanates from various transmitting sites on and from within our very planet. Most diabolical is that the virus corrupting God's divine program has also been encoded into our own DNA, warping it all in such a way that we are somehow biologically enmeshed with the projection itself. This is so far beyond my own understanding of things that it's difficult for even I to explain this coherently here. Luckily, my channel, Pep, and I have agreed to research this more, as others have done and detail the full intricacy of the illusion in our next collaboration.

The human body has been, many times, referred to as a temple. This reference is more than metaphor. The human body is literally an edifice, a bio-vehicle that houses and protects the light of the soul, our little piece of God. It is designed with high tech antennas meant to receive and transmit communication with God. These receivers are stock parts to our temples and they can be disrupted by various support mechanisms within the illusion. Among these; the various foods, drinks and corrosive additives we consume (including sugars and other poisons), DNA hacking and corruption, petty human drama and white noise, cultural mores, race wars, religions, psychiatry, medicines and immunizations ... so many ways that we are all kept in check by the one with real power, he who herds us like cattle, controlling us through the illusion we fully accept as reality.

Mesmerized by the illusion we are born into, the Man in Black controls every aspect of our lives with absolutes that we believe to be the only truth. Lost within these absolutes, our connection with our creator is cut and we are diminished. Faith in the illusion has trained us to see limits to our existence and our potential. Thus, we are controlled in life then, so hypnotized, the light which is our soul is harvested and enslaved forever by the Man in Black.

DONA JULIA'S PELUQUERIA

I walked into the Peluqueria alone. It was dark inside, a candle burning at a counter by a barber's stool, its dancing light reflecting off a mirror. The smell of sweet smelling white sage permeated the air.

At first, I thought the place was empty. Then, I saw her eyes, two disembodied white orbs materializing in the darkness. By flickering candlelight, I saw her emerge from the shadows, her twisted physique cloaked in a dark robe, her wrinkled features shrouded by a hood. Standing by the barber's stool she raised a mangled arthritic hand and beckoned me to take a seat. In her other hand she waved a razor-sharp pair of cutting shears.

Dona Julia

I first met Dona Julia in the small Mexican village of Tequisquipan when I was eleven years old. That was the summer of 1971, when my mother and Horace, my soon to be stepfather, threw both my sister and myself in the back of a 1969 Chevy Nova and we embarked on a life altering trek through Mexico.

My mother was pursuing her doctorate at U.C.L.A. and built her thesis around an exploration of the elements of folklore and legend in Mexico. Together with Horace, who, as a kid, I saw as a bold and adventurous explorer, we spent three months roughing it out of our car and in quaint posadas, going from town to town, collecting ghostly tales all over Mexico.

Whatever town or village we drove into, my mother would immediately locate its oldest and most colorful denizens, the keepers of culture, the guardians of tradition, the most celebrated storytellers. I've traveled all over the world since then, lived many places, seen many wonderful things but, to this day, that one trip through Mexico remains one of my most magical memories. On that trip, I fell in love with my mother's Mexico, the Mexico she adored; its folklore and the storytellers we met on the way.

Upon arriving in Tequisquiapan, my mother drove directly to City Hall where she immediately made the acquaintance of the Chief of Police. She explained to him her purpose and he led us directly to the tiny home of Dona Julia.

Dona Julia was very old. How old? I don't think anyone knew for sure. She must have been in her late eighties at least, crippled by arthritis and blind. At first, I was scared by this weird, troll-like little woman but, as I listened to her tell my mother her stories, I became entranced by her vibrant youthful spirit. Although her body was misshapen by various ailments she seemed to prance about like a little girl and while she was blind - her eyes were white and round as ping pong balls - she navigated her surroundings as well as anyone with sight.

The story behind her physical afflictions was known throughout town, her story itself a fixture of local myth and legend.

Julia grew up very poor. Her father was the town drunk and was known to all as a laughing stock. One day, however, her father returned home surprisingly sober with wealth beyond belief. Soon after, her family moved into a luxurious hacienda on the outskirts of town and her father was elected mayor, a position he held for many years.

She was just a child when, on one night, very late, Julia heard her father leave the house on one of his many mysterious night trips. She often wondered where her father was going so late and she was also very curious about the gold he would return with.

On this particular evening, she decided to follow her father. She trailed behind him high into the wild dark hills and came upon a clearing where she saw her father signing the dark leather-bound book of a man dressed in black. While she had never seen this Man in Black before, she knew of him. He was the man that the viejos told the children of the village to always avoid, the Man in Black that lived in the dark hills surrounding Tequisquiapan. He was, the viejos warned, the devil.

On her way home, racing to get back home before her father, she became lost in the darkness. Tripping over a branch, she fell, face first, into the mud. Rising, she saw the Man in Black now standing before her, his dark book in his gloved hands. A hood hung over his head, obscuring his features, but with a slight tilt of his head, Julia caught a glimpse of his scaled reptilian skin and bug-like eyes in the moonlight.

"I see through you," she said bravely, refusing to give up her soul by signing his book. "I know who you are."

"Do you?" he replied with a snakelike hiss.

Dropping his book to the mud and taking her hands into his, the Man in Black pulled close to Julia. She looked into his shroud, this time seeing only a deep dark void of nothingness. She closed her eyes now as he drew her into that darkness and felt his hard, cold reptilian lips kiss each of her eye lids.

"Child," she heard him taunt in the darkness, "you will see no more!"

He embraced her, his hold so strong that she was powerless to squirm. Then there was nothing. Three days later, the townspeople, who had mobilized to find the missing child, discovered her unconscious on the trail, blind, twisted and crippled.

I was amazed now to find Dona Julia here, on the Boulevard of the Dead. I knew her for only a day or so but her influence upon me was lifelong. Dona Julia's tales haunted me; stories of duendes, ghosts and demons. They are the stories of my childhood, my mother's stories, the stories I told my own kids and which my grandchild will grow up hearing. Her impact upon me was so great in fact that she exists in various incarnations in the many stories I have written. Whether as Julia, Abuelita or as a curandera, anyone with enough spare time, or bizarre interest, to rummage through my dusty files and read the tales I've penned will surely find the presence of a magical, blind and arthritic old sage woven into the fabric of each story.

"Have a seat," Dona Julia said, spinning the stool so that the seat faced me.

I sat, and Dona Julia wrapped what I thought was an old white sheet around me to catch the falling snippets of hair. Instantly, she spun me around so that I faced the mirror. I was surprised by the person I saw reflected in the glass.

In the mirror, candlelight glistening in a golden aura around me and shimmering off the glass, I saw myself draped in the blue feathered robes of what I thought be a Mayan high priest.

Quetzal feathers, of course.

They were the same ornate robes worn by the old painter in my childhood dreams.

Similar to the robes adorned by your father in his own lucid dreams. Again, reflections of glorious past lives.

Somewhere in the shadows of that peluqueria, my jaguar growled. Now, also reflected in that mirror, I saw Julia's white eyes hovering above my shoulder. Over the other shoulder, I saw the cutting shears just inches from my ear.

"How do you want your hair?" she asked.

Before I could respond, she had already begun. She whipped her shears around my head in a blur, cutting furiously so that bits and pieces of my hair popped everywhere about my head. At first,

I was nervous she would snip off an ear or poke my eyes with the razor sharp blades but I soon relaxed and became mesmerized by her magical dexterity and amazing skill. Out of breath, she finally lowered her shears.

"Behold," she declared, "You!"

I looked into the mirror. Rather than short and fresh cut, my hair was now long and flowing beneath a headdress of iridescent blue feathers. They were the same blue quetzal feathers that made up the bristles of the old painter's brushes and that now adorned my robes. *As the quetzal bird represented liberty to the Mayans, the Quetzal is a light-sonic frequency liberating mankind from the lies of the Man in Black. Tuning into the quetzal connects us with our creator, the great masculine/feminine duality we know as God. These quetzal birds are usually green, but for you...they are blue.*

"It is you. The you that you dreamed of. The you I see that you cannot. The you that you chose to be in Heaven."

"You can't see," I blurted, speaking to Dona Julia's reflection in the mirror.

She laughed, a sort of cackle, actually. Grabbing a broom from the wall she began sweeping up the hair on the floor.

"I see better than you," she answered, brushing the hair into a little pile and by a dark corner, "through the illusion of the Man in Black."

Dona Julia pointed across the dark shop to a waiting area where there was a musty couch, a plant and a magazine rack. On the couch, I saw, once again, the little boy who was once me. He was a tad older now, maybe eleven, and he sat there as he had in the panaderia, drawing.

Dona Julia nudged me out of my seat towards the boy. Looking over his shoulder, I caught a peak at what he was drawing.

The boy was drawing in pencil on a coarse Bristol board designed for pen and ink. It was a picture of one of the great heroes of my childhood, Emiliano Zapata, a great leader of the Mexican Revolution, riding atop his white horse. Scattered about the boy's lap was other half-finished drawings of Aztec warriors, crosses and even a rough sketch of a catholic church.

The boy finished shading in Zapata's big black mustache then, suddenly, looked up at me.

"Do you remember?" the boy asked.

You were beginning to remember many things you had blocked out for years.

"Do you remember?" Dona Julia repeated as if in echo.

I remembered sitting in the back seat of the Nova for nearly three months on the road. I stared out the window, my mother behind the wheel and Horace resting his head on her lap with his bare feet sticking out the passenger window, as an endless arid landscape, road signs, cacti and the occasional cross whizzed by. Those crosses were propped up in memoriam to those who lost their lives on those highways.

I recalled how I passed the infinite hours on the road, imagining a dark rider on a white stallion galloping breakneck alongside our car. Sometimes, this rider, a black-clad Charro, would disappear behind a passing slope or some brush, an underpass or tunnel but he would always reappear on the open road. He was always there whenever we took to the highways, the landscape a blur behind him, like a guardian angel watching over me and my family. Spiriting through the heat waves in the distance I also saw the jade jaguar tracking us as we sped along the highway.

The wide brim of the Charro's sombrero kept his features always in shadow, but here and there, I was able to catch a fleeting glimpse of his face, when he'd tip his head to look at me and the sun hit just right. But, it wasn't Zapata's face I'd see. It was always my own. It was always me.

It was you.

The warrior.

The revolutionary.

I remembered now. I wanted to be like Zapata. I wanted to be a great warrior. I wanted to be the one who ushered in momentous change – to free people from oppression. As Zapata fought for land and liberty, I now wanted to fight for something right and noble.

Now, in the classroom, on the court and with this first and most humble book, you fight in your own way with millions of enlightened others to bring about a paradigm shift; one of many warriors in the revolution to free men's souls from the oppression of the Man in Black's malevolent illusion. Through your collective efforts, all people might someday see through the fog and into the light.

There was, even at eleven, a very urgent and truly romantic desire to rise and take a stand against evil. As a kid I was prone to romanticize things. My father in me, I suppose. My mother, too. As much as I fantasized about fighting diabolical forces, it really was all in my head. In truth, I hated to fight. I detested the base and dismal thumping sounds of bare fists against the skull. I avoided fighting as much as possible. That's not to say that I didn't get into my fair share of scrapes growing up or that I couldn't hold my own with my fists when I truly felt the need.

"Only fight," my father lectured, after I beat up a kid in elementary school simply for making fun of my nickname, "if you are willing to kill or if you are willing to die."

My nickname, among my family and friends, was Pep. Not one day passed in all my years of schooling, when some kid didn't make fun of that name in some way, calling me, Pippi Longstalking, Pepperoni or Pee Pee.

For the most part, I put up with all the teasing, just as I would in high school. Still, on one bad day, in sixth grade, I snapped when Alfredo, the first of many bullies I would encounter in my life, called me Pee Pee.

It is no small wonder that you detest bullying today and that you work so hard to end bullying of any kind.

After placing Alfredo in a headlock, I threw him to the ground, driving his head into the asphalt. I still cringe at the memory of the dead clunk that came with Alfredo's head hitting the blacktop. The fight ended instantly with Alfredo nearly unconscious. Of course, I was sent to the principal who immediately contacted my father.

Arriving home, I expected my father to be proud of his young warrior. Instead, he was very upset.

"Always respect your opponent," my father continued, "you never know who he really is or what cause he may be fighting for. You don't know if he's a black belt or how far he is willing to take the fight, if he is willing to kill. When you fight, you need to be ready to kill or die. Would you have been willing to die because this boy called you Pee Pee? Would you be able to live with yourself, knowing that you killed because someone called you a name? Make sure, the next time that you fight, that your reason for fighting is a good one, something you can't walk away from."

The Man in Black is a bully.

Yes, he is.

You know what he wants.

I do. It is a fight that I cannot walk away from.

A fight you are willing to live or die for?

Yes.

Your father would be proud.

Those who fight for the Quetzal battle upon spiritual battlefields; scars seared into their hearts and souls.

The boy's drawings spurred new memories of a love for history born within me that magical summer, exploring the ruins of Teotihuacan, Monte Alban, Chichen Itza and, especially, the Mayan city of Palenque. How my imagination soared, how connected I felt to history there, to the ghosts of those people who walked these ancient sites before me.

You were there before in a past life. You walked with these ghosts. I was there with you.

And then there were the churches, Mother Mary and stories of miracles and mystical healings. Today, I am no great fan of the Catholic Church and I view all organized religions as tools of the Man in Black's intricate mass deception. But, I admit my fascination with Catholicism as a boy. I was awestruck by the ornate grandeur and monolithic size of the churches built by the Spanish all over Mexico. I was greatly taken by the symbols of Christianity; of the cross, saints and, especially, of the Virgen De Guadalupe. I was so awestruck by all of this that I thought, perhaps, I was being called to the priesthood. Maybe this was the way I could make my heroic stand against evil.

It was not the Catholic church calling but something much higher. It was the beckoning call of the Creator, the great all father and mother

duality, that you heard. You just didn't recognize it yet. As I said, you didn't know who you were. Your memories of a past life and of another, higher order of priesthood was still blocked.

I have no doubt that I was being divinely called to some form of priesthood, albeit not the Catholic kind, and to a life of service. *The life of a teacher and one who paints the world blue.*

I waffled back and forth, depending on the day, with my aspirations. One day I was convinced God wanted me to lead the next Mexican Revolution. On another, I dreamed about directing epic motion pictures. The next day, I daydreamed about the lazy life of a happy friar, sipping on apricot brandy and living the good life.

There was one thing I was certain about, however. I knew that; whether as a warrior battling evil, a storyteller or a priest; that I wanted to save the world and free people from evil. I always knew that I wanted to save and heal people. I wanted to be like the White Shadow.

More like a Brown Shadow.

★ ★

"Remember?" I heard Dona Julia ask again.

"I do."

She smiled as I turned toward her, one or two yellowed teeth protruding through sickly gray gums. Behind her, I saw again my reflection in the mirror, an aura of blue light radiating all about me.

"You do," she was pleased to sense, "I see that you remember your dreams now."

I dreamed of being a warrior and a priest, an artist and an athlete, a teacher and a coach.

She grunted, tapping her mangled fist against her forehead, then against her chest then lifting it, opened and warped, above her head.

The salute of the Ghost Warrior.

Candlelight flickered wildly now so that twisted shapes and shadows danced madly about the walls.

Dona Julia then delivered to me a, by now, familiar message. Though it was her mouth that moved, it was the voice of the old painter that I heard.

"You have been blessed with many brushes to fight the battle for God against the forces of the Man in Black."

Again, I heard the growl of my jaguar nagual, followed by the familiar warm rush.

"Brushes? How can I fight with brushes?"

"You'll paint the world blue," Dona Julia responded, her own voice returned to her, "and in that blue draw enslaved souls into the Quetzal and deliver them to Heaven. Set them free. In that, the Man in Black will be defeated."

Glancing back, I saw that the boy was no longer there. A new rush of warm energy streamed within me and left me with the sense that I would not see him again. He left his drawings behind, however.

"Your dream," Dona Julia whispered, "is your purpose. What is your dream?"

Looking into the mirror, my priestly robes and headdress still glowing blue, it all seemed so clear. Yes, I dreamed of making movies, writing books, telling stories, teaching, coaching. In that moment, though, I felt an even higher purpose in it all.

"I think," I began.

"You think?" Dona Julia interrupted.

"I know…I feel, that I want to be a healer, a liberator of souls, a warrior-priest."

"You are a storyteller," Dona Julia responded with a weird twitch of her white eyes.

"I am."

"You are a healer."

"I am."

"You are a warrior."

"I am."

"You are a liberator of souls."

"I am."

"You are a high priest and all of these things and also…a creator."

"I am."

"These are your brushes."

Aware now of the Man in Black's illusion you would now also grow to become more sensitive of your own divine capacity to manifest your dreams in this life…through the Quetzal.

Dona Julia laughed with gleeful approval, tapping the seat, inviting me to sit again. The feathers on my robe fluttered within the bright blue aura.

"Now," she said, "you are beginning to see."

"See?"

"Who you are."

Taking my seat, she spun me around so that we faced each other through our reflections in the mirror.

"Seeing true and through the illusion," she explained, "requires that you be able to listen."

"To what?"

"For your own *voice* in all the noise. Find your voice, be bold to follow it and you'll see through his lies and find your purpose."

"What lies exactly are we talking about?"

Her white eyes glowed brighter now, with a pulsing bright intensity, as she leaned over my shoulder to whisper in my ear.

"Beware the Man in Black," she whispered.

"He's real?" I asked.

"Live your dream and you'll see through his deception," she instructed, nodding, "live out the purpose that you chose for yourself and you'll lead others past his illusion too. Fulfill your purpose and you can help others see through the lies that limit them from realizing who they are and what they are here to do. You are a warrior-priest, one of many leaders in the revolution that is soon to come. Your stories, your art, your teaching and even your coaching are among the many brushes you wield to fight the Man in Black. These brushes are your weapons."

Revolution? What was this old blind woman telling me, I thought, and why was she telling me at all?

★ ★

Before the Boulevard of the Dead, you had your own brief encounter with the Man in Black.

Or, one among his legions who came to do his evil will.

Although you didn't know him by name, you sensed his malevolence. Remember?

I saw him in Tucson, with Jake, at the traditional Indian medicine seminar.

You felt his power.

We all did.

In the ballroom of a now defunct Ramada Inn in Tucson, Arizona, we gathered in a massive circle. We sat, people from all over the world, those like me looking to be healed and those who were there to learn the art of healing. Outside, a great December storm raged; rain pounding against the windows, thunder clamoring and lightning flashing.

There must have been 200 people in the ballroom, maybe more, the Medicine Man standing at the center, preparing to deliver a most important lecture on Unconditional Love. Although we were indoors and while it was raining outside, the Medicine Man nevertheless sported his dark shades. I cannot remember a time that whole week when he wasn't wearing his sunglasses or holding a cigarette in his hands.

Suddenly, the entrance doors flew open, rain and debris blowing into the room. We all sat stunned as a huge Native American man dressed in black leather barged into the ballroom, broke the sacred circle in which we were all aligned and marched into the center where he squared off with the Medicine Man.

You all knew not to break the sacred circle as it had been blessed with prayers and sage.

No one knew who this mammoth man dressed all in black was or why he came. He stood no less than 6'5" and must have weighed near 300 pounds. We knew he was bad.

He came to disrupt.

The two men said nothing as they stood motionless at the center of the broken circle. There was an uneasy stillness in the grand ballroom, as the silent tension between these two men began to build. While there were no words spoken nor one fist raised, there was something dark and heavy going on between these men. A battle waged.

A spiritual battle, a fight no one in that room could see but could certainly feel. This Man in Black was here to stop the Medicine Man from doing his good work that day.

It was then that the Medicine Man pulled off his sunglasses for the first and only time, at least as far as I knew, that entire week.

Staring hard into the Man in Black's eyes, he maintained his stoic, hard expression. Still, neither man made a move nor stepped away. While nothing seemed to be happening, the tension in the room was electric. **This battle was between the powers of good and evil.**

Finally, the Man in Black, dropped his shoulders and retreated backwards, almost stumbling, flashing a furious look at the Medicine Man before turning and taking off outside, back into the storm from which he came. He was defeated...

On that one day, good won out. But the devil is a resilient one.

The Medicine Man put his glasses back on.

★ ★

I heard the growl of my jaguar and the peluqueria went suddenly black. In the darkness I still felt the old woman's presence about me, her warped hands clutching my shoulders and her warm breath on my ear as I heard her whisper once again, "beware the Man in Black. He is real." **I told you.**

OLD PAINTER'S GALLERY 4

THE MAN IN BLACK

The Battle for Heaven
There exists only the creator and the created

God, whatever God is to you, created all that is.

For me, God is a great creative duality, composed of a harmonious balance of masculine and feminine aspects. Elohim. It is this creative duality that creates all that is, just as it takes man and woman to bring forth life on Earth, it only makes sense to me that the greatest creative force, that which created all that is, would also have masculine and feminine aspects.

All that is not God, God created. We are all creations of God. As are Angels.

Among these angels there was one, highly ranked and beloved, who was jealous of God's power and who wanted to be God. This angel led others in a war to dethrone God and take God's place in what we believe to be Heaven. This angel, known as Lucifer, lost this war and retreated, with what was left of his rebel legions, his demons, to Earth.

With him, also, Lucifer took hostage many of God's most precious and most adored creations, human beings - trapping them on Earth within an illusion designed to harvest the light from within them. This light is their souls. It is the light of creation itself, each drop of light, a divine piece to a greater more incomprehensible whole, a lumninous bit of God. The more light Lucifer can harvest the more powerful he believes he will become, the more he will be like God. And that is Lucifer's goal – to become more like God. To replace God.

Within this illusion, Lucifer employs a variety of mecahnisms of deception that keep men locked into the illusion and detached from God. In this most real sense, Earth is Hell.

God still reaches out to save his beloved creations from eternal damnation. Once, 2,000 years ago, God came in human form to save man's souls, to let us know the manifesting power that all men and women share to commune with the divine and thus create their destinies – power that Lucifer blinds us all to within the fog of his illusion. Lucifer is the Man in Black.

Lucifer harvests the light after our death to reproduce his own life forms just as God recycles light –so too does Lucifer plan to become more powerful. God nevertheless tries to reach out and retreive the light so lost and bring it all back to Heaven.

It is a war for light. There is a good and and there is a bad. And we are the warriors, we are the ones leading the revolution to expose the illusion, through love, disciplined meditative practice and lifestyle change, we will see the truth and we will reconnect with the divine frequency of our creator.

RIVER OF THE DAMNED

The next thing I knew, I was standing by the ledge of a bridge, fog crushing in around me. A horn blared behind me, scaring me so soundly that I nearly leapt over the rail. Catching my breath, I heard the old painter cackling joyously behind me. I turned to see him, again sitting in the passenger seat of my red Honda Civic. He opened the door and stepped outside with me.

I now recognized this bridge as the Pagaro Bridge, just outside of Loma, not far from my fatal crash and still within the immediate vicinity of the Boulevard of the Dead. Below me I could hear the rumble of raging waters.

"Nice haircut," the old painter casually remarked, leaning lazily against the rail of the bridge, "the old lady really has an eye for a good trim." He directed me closer to the bridge's edge and pointed to the water below. Beneath me I could see a rush of dark water pouring torrential through the underpass, clashing helter-skelter against the rocks, a mangled flood of mud, twisted roots, trees and debris.

The surge of water below me sent tremors throughout the bridge. Within the roar of the enraged torrent passing beneath us, I heard, or thought I heard, an agonized chorus of wails.

The River of the Damned

The cries of millions of suffering souls.

Looking down at the dark rapids I could see a mass of silhouetted figures drowning in the flood, fighting the hammering currents, their mouths stretched grotesque as they gasped for air, dark arms with fingers outstretched reaching out for help that was not there.

Initially, I wanted to jump over the rail, dive into the rush of dark water and help but I held myself back; there were too many to save. The currents were so strong that the victims were swept beneath the bridge too quickly for me to gauge them. Their agonized wails grew louder and louder, their cries pulsing within the very fog that blanketed us.

As the cries intensified, I found that the numbers of those who were drowning within the wild dark waters multiplied. Below me, a gelatinous mesh of dark flesh, people, both deformed and formless, stuck or somehow melded together in a weird blackened liquid form, almost like tar, shrieking bodies pounding violent, crashing, almost splashing against the rocky river banks. If, indeed, I was touring the Boulevard of the Dead, surely, I thought, this must be the River of the Damned.

Louder and louder the cries became, so loud, in fact, that I couldn't think and pressing my hands tightly against my ears did nothing to drown out this horrible clamor. Then, through the maddening racket, I somehow heard his voice.

"Pep," the old painter whispered, and his whisper cut through all the calamity, all the noise, "hear my voice."

Then, all was suddenly silent; a silence so pure, so still. They were still down there, every one of them doomed, still reaching and clawing desperately, mouths agape in, what was now, muted horrific anticipation of their fates. They were as sewage carried out to sea, poor souls flushed to oblivion.

"What is this?" I asked, "Who are they?"

"Damned to Hell."

"They're going to Hell?"

"Damned to Earth. Earth is Hell."

This River of the Damned teems with those who have lost their souls to the Man in Black's illusion, those who could not see nor hear their own voices in the din of his noise and diversion.

"He is the Devil," the old painter continued, "Just as Dona Julia said and He wants your soul. He wants all of our souls."

I stepped carefully away from the rail of the bridge, fearful of falling over.

"Earth is His place. His illusion. Our Hell."

The Man in Black's illusion is the world that we think is real. A world fixated on petty human dramas and material concerns. A projection orchestrated by The Man in Black and supported by his demons and a multitude of instruments of deception.

The subject of my next book, of course.

The Man in Black harvests those souls addicted to His illusion, those who have invested their faith in His projection of reality, those who have lost their connection with the Quetzal. They are the zombies who have unknowingly surrendered their souls to Him, the diabolical reaper of souls. Only by tuning into the Quetzal can we hope to avoid this River of the Damned and escape the Hell that awaits.

Find your voice outside the noise and distraction of His illusion and you will find God reaching out to you in the Quetzal and, in God, find yourself.

The old painter looked into the menacing fog, pointing a finger to the far end of the bridge leading back to the Boulevard of the Dead.

"Listen for your own voice," he smiled, "and you will …see the light."

There, somewhere deep and far within the fog, somewhere, radiating, from the most remote corner of the Boulevard of the Dead, at the end of the road, I saw a flicker, a pin prick of white light piercing through the dark and heavy mist.

"I see it now," I said, feeling comforted by the sight, "I see the light you're talking about. I see Heaven."

You were now tuning into the Quetzal. You were beginning to see through the fog of the Man in Black's illusion, beginning to hear your own voice. I told you at the beginning of our little joyride that your death was a blessing. Well, what greater blessing than the opportunity to save your soul by recognizing that which is real from that which is not?

"How do I know this is real?" I asked the old painter as bright shafts of white light began to cut through the fog in the distance, "How do I know this is not a dream, that I'm not crazy, that I really am *listening* to my own voice and that what I'm thinking is real?"

The old painter turned calmly toward me. Despite the ghastly tumult below us, all was still and silent.

The Medicine Man taught us that it's not about what you're thinking.

"It's about how we feel," the old painter reminded, "does it feel right?"

I took that moment to gauge just that. I closed my eyes and took in a deep breath, letting the air out slowly. I felt no anxiety or sense of fear in my belly, no butterflies about any of this at all. It all felt right to me, everything the old painter said. It all felt real, it all felt right.

"You know you have found yourself" the old painter continued, "because, here I am. I am your guardian angel."

Here we are.

"THE WISE ONE"
A LITTLE GIRL IN GARLANDS

At one point along the way, I found myself in a field of thick fog and high grass. While I didn't see them, I sensed that the old painter and my jaguar were nearby. I could hear their footsteps over dry leaves, somewhere in the mist.

Then, two figures materialized, hand in hand, in the fog before me. One was an indistinguishable silhouette, graceful and lean. If not for such a youthful vibrancy about this obscure fellow, I would have taken him to be my father. To be sure, he had his energy, a certain panache to his posture, a polish in his stance, but I just couldn't be sure. As I've said, my father was sixty when I was born and while he carried his boyish nature well into his eighties, he was an old man for as long as I knew him. I never saw him as young so, to this day, I can't be sure that the dark and stylish outline that came to me in that field was my father or not. I can say, though, that I think it might have been.

It was.

He came to me, this elegant silhouette, as if to deliver a gift and that gift came holding his hand in the shape of a little girl, no more than four or five, a little girl with garlands in her long curly brown hair. Unlike him, she came in very clear.

Her face was exquisite and pristine as a china doll, with wondrous wide eyes the color of chocolate. Just a child, there was a certain knowing about her dark brown eyes that led me somehow to know that I was in the presence of a very old and wise soul.

"She has the soul of a wise one," I heard the old painter whisper from somewhere in the fog, "she is coming to teach you how to love." *Unconditional Love. One of the Seven Sacred Aspects; loving ourselves and others simply because we are all of the same bright source. Your daughter, Rosemarie, came to teach you to love... simply because."*
Being a parent would prove a lifelong lesson in letting go. Rosemarie would grow up to be a handful. Outspoken, opinionated and fiercely independent, she would test and challenge you and cut her own path. She would be one that you would love and sacrifice for but would never control.

The little wise one, with colorful garlands in her hair, gave me a wave and a smile before both she and the lean silhouette disappeared within the rolling fog.

I would see those eyes again soon upon my return to the Land of the Living. I would recognize that same wise old soul in the light glimmering from my baby daughter's chocolate colored eyes that following March. I would name her, upon my mother's suggestion, Rosemarie, the wise one.

One day, holding Rosemarie in my arms, rocking her to sleep, looking deep into her big brown eyes before they closed, a lullaby came to me. *It came to you through me.*

I sang this song to her every night that I laid her to bed as a child and whenever she would let me as a teen. I'm sure to haunt her with it in her dreams, humming it in her ear as I pass through the Boulevard of the Dead, again, on my way to Heaven. It goes like this;

"You're the wise one,
My teeny little wise one,
You're the wise one, little Rosemarie.
People will be coming from far away,
Just to hear what you have to say.
With your magic, magic eyes,
You can see through people's lies.
You can see into their hearts,
And heal them up, every part.
You're the wise one,
My teeny little wise one,

You can see what I cannot.
You can see all the world's magic
And you see it with your heart.
You're the wise one,
My teeny little wise one,
You're the wise one,
Little Rosemarie.

Rosemarie would certainly prove to be a wise one, an old soul, a young lady older than her years. From the time she was teeny she had that special insight to the other side.

During that full year of our separation, before our predictable divorce, my wife slept in the bedroom and I on the couch. Every morning, at about 5, Rosemarie would wake up and find her way from her bedroom onto the couch where she would sleep with me until I woke up for work.

One morning, as she lay wide awake beside me, I heard her let out what I can only describe as a happy gasp. I opened my eyes to see her sitting up and, giddy, pointing up at the ceiling.

"I saw angels," she told me, "they were right there, smiling at me."

She was only four when she saw her first angels. From the beginning, Rosemarie was able to perceive things that no one else around her could. **Unlike you, she embraced the angels that came to her. She was unafraid.**

One day, when Rosemarie was four years old, the two of us took a long hike through the redwoods of Marks Park, near our home. It is a place my grown children fondly remember today as the Dorothy Woods because of how it reminded them of the Emerald Forest in the *Wizard of Oz*. Many times, I took them there, searching for Bigfoot, talking about ghosts and fairies and enjoying the magic of nature.

Sitting by a creek, one day, as soft streaks of sunlight blended mystically with the trees, we rested along the trail and sat quietly by a running stream. Here, so quiet and still, we listened to the babble of water and ruffling of leaves in the high trees.

"Daddy," Rosemarie asked, "what is the water saying?"

She already sensed the spirit in all things, that all things whether animal, tree or rock were alive.

I listened for a moment to the babble of the stream then responded with I don't know, my love, what do you think it is saying?

"It says 'keep me clean. Take care of me and save me.'"

A tender breeze rattled some branches above us and leaves drifted from the trees, landing quietly upon the running stream.

"What are the trees saying, daddy?" Rosemarie continued.

"Tell me, Rosemarie, what are they saying?"

"The trees are saying 'take care of us.'"

I can never know why, in the spirit world before she was born, Rosemarie chose me as her father. That is for her to remember. I am convinced, however, that I chose her as a lesson in love and in loving enough to let go. Rosemarie was 13 when she let me know with no uncertainty that Dad, I love you but I'm not you. Rosemarie was blessed with a fearless eye and ear for angels, spirits and her own voice. Much bolder than I was at her age.

If that was my father I saw in that mist sopped field, offering me a glimpse of blessings to come, it would not be the last time I would see him on the Boulevard of the Dead. He would come to me again, very soon, and with other gifts.

The Little Girl in Garlands

OLD PAINTER'S GALLERY 5

THE VOICE

In our heads we hear many voices – the voices of our families, our friends, our enemies, sometimes the Man in Black himself. They are the voices of those who, themselves are either lost in the illusion or who control the illusion. These voices are meant to crush our own. These voices diminish us so that we fall prey to fear, guilt, hate, anger and all forms of insecurities.

In this the Man in Black keeps us all in line, so we never discover our divine origins. These voices are very loud, so loud that most of us can't even discern our own voices from the voices of others. So clamorous are these voices that we actually think we are thinking what we think we are thinking. These voices, many times, determine our self-worth, our grasp on reality. They define for us who we really are which, as you know, is not at all who we really are.

Our own voice, our highest self, that light and bit of God, which we really are is drowned out by the flood and clamor of a zillion other voices – so that we may never know the truth about our identities. Indeed, why would the Man in Black, who can only grow stronger by harvesting our souls, our light, want us to know that we are all connected to God and, in that, equipped with all the power necessary to, not only manifest our every dream but also soundly defeat him? Why would he want us aware of our own divinity? Why?

We find our voice within the Quetzal and that voice is both our own and God's. We are all one.

Meditate on this. Let all the voices play themselves out, sit quietly and wait patiently for your own voice to call out to you. You will recognize it, you will know the truth for it will feel right and settled in your stomach. Listen for your voice and the calling will come. You will know what your life's purpose is, your mission will be clear. You will remember your dreams and be called again to fight for them. It is never toolate. It is God's will.

THE LA REINA THEATER

When I was a kid, there were two special havens I would escape to when the pressures of my young life became such that I felt compelled to vanish. My very favorite place to run to and hide out in, outside my own bedroom of course, my own fortress of solitude when I was eleven, was the old La Reina Theater. Here, I would flee from the world and indulge the life I lived in my head.

The old La Reina Theater on Ventura Boulevard in Sherman Oakes, California, was just down the street from the Del Valle Apartments and the two-bedroom dwelling my sister and I shared with my mother after the divorce.

Today, the interior of that quaint little theater has been gutted and converted into a shopping mall, although the original marquis sign still stands. In 1971, the La Reina Theater was like a second home to me. I spent nearly every summer day, weekends and holidays there. On most summer weekdays, the theater would be empty, and I would have it all to myself. For 75 cents, I would walk through the lobby at 10 in the morning and stay until dinner time every day, slipping comfortably into the back seats, retreating into the soothing darkness which seemed almost to drape about me like a warm comforter, and immerse myself, (indeed, astral project myself) into the movie screen.

It was in the La Reina where my love for film was born, where my desire to tell stories with pictures was ignited. I saw *Butch Cassidy and the Sundance Kid* twenty-two times in one week, *Willy Wonka and the Chocolate Factory* five times a day for two weeks and a *James Bond triple feature of Dr. No, From Russia with Love and Goldfinger* from morning to night for a month. That was pretty much the case for every film that came to the La Reina. From *True Grit* to *the Godfather, Bullitt, Death Wish, Dirty Harry* to *The Hot Rock, What's Up Doc?* and *It's a Mad, Mad, Mad, Mad World.* I saw them all over and over and over again.

Like I said, there was no place, outside my own bedroom where I felt more at home. Even today, outside of a basketball gymnasium, the enchanted redwood trails of the Dorothy Woods, or Meditation Mount in Ojai, there is no place I'd rather be than in a movie theater.

There is another place...

Cochise's Stronghold, sixty miles outside of Tucson, a magical place, to be sure. To this most powerful and sacred spot, I've made my pilgrimage on several occasions, usually with Jake as my guide, when I needed to escape the world and when my prayers were most urgent.

It is said that the remains of Cochise, the great Apache chief, are buried somewhere within this mazelike terrain of jagged rocks, high peaks and treacherous gorges, protected by the spirits. There has never been a time, on any of my visits here, when something supernatural or exquisite did not occur.

It is a magical place.

★ ★

Our apartment was small. Even before Horace entered our lives, there weren't enough rooms for the three of us so my mother, newly divorced, took the living room and slept on a couch. That way my sister and I could have our own bedrooms. It was typical of my mother to sleep on a couch so that we could have beds and our own rooms. She always made every sacrifice for our safety and comfort. Although we were poor, she somehow found a way to spoil us.

No other kid I knew, whether in the modest Del Valle complex, a kind of retreat for divorced single mothers, in which we rented a two-bedroom apartment, or Beverly Hills, was lavished with as many gifts as we were on Christmas mornings. It might be that the small size of our living room made it look like we had more than we actually did but waking up to see a sparkling Christmas tree towering above mountains of gifts spread all about the floor brought a great and magical, if material, climax to all the anticipation building up to Christmas morning. Easter was not much different as we would wake up each year to a giant hollowed ceramic egg stuffed with the finest Allen Wertz candies. My mother always went all out for us, doing the best that she could to give us a normal childhood despite the financial obstacles we encountered.

As kids, we never know the hoops our parents jump through for us. It is only now, as a father, that I can fully appreciate the sacrifices my mother and Horace both made for us.

"I don't care how little we have," my mother would say, "you'll never have less than anyone else. You'll always have what everyone else has."

And, we did. My mother always made it happen – though, to make it happen she struggled through two jobs while also working on her doctorate.

You were never spoiled. It was more than just gifts. You were loved. The gifts were never a substitution for her time or her love. Gifts were an added bonus. You always got more and through her love you were taught to appreciate all that you received. Through her love you were taught to give.

My Other Mother

Nevertheless, as loved as I was, the times before Horace entered our lives were tough for a bashful latchkey kid without a dad at home to wrestle or to play catch with and a mother who spent most days and nights working. Sometimes, I like to romanticize and think that I actually had two mothers. My birth mother, of course, the one who raised me, suffered and sacrificed for me, the one who was there to feed me and care for me, who spoiled me at Christmas, Easter and my birthday.

My other mother, however, was a television set. I often joke that I was raised by a television. If not necessarily my mother, TV was at the very least a great babysitter

As I said, my sister and I were very much latchkey kids of the seventies. My mother attended U.C.L.A during the day, while we were in school and worked for a spell as a Ranchera singing waitress at a local Mexican restaurant, at night. While she sent us to school each morning with a hearty bacon and egg breakfast, she was rarely home when we returned from school and in the summer we were on our own every day to take care of ourselves. The 1970's was a simpler era than the crazy times of our present day. Mothers didn't always know where their kids were during the day but thee was a confidence that they were nevertheless safe. As long as they were home for dinner, there was no cause for alarm. The world was a little safer, we thought, back then.

I spent most of my time alone, drawing on my bed, watching television. I loved my TV. I was not, however, an average couch potato. The hours I spent in front of the black and white tube, even at eleven, were not wasted. Indeed, I was studying. I was a student of film, of story, of acting, dialogue, editing and cinematography. I studied all the great directors and recognized their style inside and out.

Television also offered me an idealized vision of the wholesome family life that I perceived to be missing in our broken home. *The Brady Bunch, Father Knows Best, The Partridge Family, Dick Van Dyke* and *Ozzie and Harriet*, offered me a glimpse of what I thought normal family life was all about and I bought into this illusion hook, line and sinker.

My interest in history was also ignited by television. If I saw the 1939 version of *The Adventures of Robin Hood,* I was compelled to study up on the real Robin Hood and to learn more about medieval England. Tyrone Power and *The Mark of Zorro* motivated me to learn about California history, just as *Dracula* inspired me to know more about Bram Stoker, Vlad Dracul and Romania.

As a history teacher, I know that the ability to teach history effectively is all in the presentation. Well, Hollywood, made a great and romanticized presentation and, with each great film, I was determined to know more about the actors, the directors, the making of the movie, the characters and... the history. A dream was born then of\ telling stories on film.

It is all a part of your divine plan. Maybe, this will be the tale that makes it to the big screen.

As in my bedroom, with the door closed and the curtains drawn, I felt safe in the La Reina. Whereas everything else in my life at that time was confusing and unpredictable, the La Reina provided me safe haven. As I said, the only place I enjoyed better than my bedroom was sitting alone in the darkness of the La Reina Theater.

It wouldn't be too difficult to imagine then how excited I was to see the La Reina marquis jutting out from the dark fog by an alleyway on the Boulevard of the \Dead.

The View from Tlalocan

Advertised on the brightly lit marquis sign was a film I had never seen nor heard of before. It was called, *The View from Tlalocan*. As I approached the box office, I saw that there was no one collecting tickets inside. There was only a cardboard sign propped up against the window that read;

"Welcome to Tlalocan."

In Aztec spirituality and legend, Tlalocan was a heaven watched over by the rain god, Tlaloc, a paradise reserved for those who died by drowning, lightning strike or leprosy.
I guess car accidents as well.

Tlalocan in a movie theater? It made perfect sense that my heaven would be to spend eternity in a movie theater. Surely, I thought, I must have lived a better life than I thought to deserve such bliss. I heard the growl of the jaguar nearby, somewhere in the darkness.

It took a few moments for my eyes to adjust to the pitch blackness of the theater. Once I could see, though, I was able to find my way to the back row of the empty theater, towards my usual spot just below the projector's booth. As a kid, I would stare upward into the glittering shaft of light that magically projected image and action onto the screen below. As I neared my familiar spot, however, I was surprised to see that my seat was already taken.

Once again, I was face to face with a younger version of myself, an eleven year old Pep dressed in loose sweats, oblivious to my presence, devouring a tub of hot buttered popcorn (in the days when it was real butter, by the way) and sipping on fruit punch. In his wanderlust eyes I saw reflected the light from the mammoth movie screen within which his whole being was now so deeply immersed.

Then, on the big screen, the old painter's face appeared in 3D on close-up.

"Please take a seat," the old painter playfully directed, "and, as a courtesy to others, please refrain from talking during the presentation of our feature."

Young Pep glanced at me with an impatient smirk, motioning for me to hush and take a seat beside him. I did as I was directed and, as I sat, the young boy just disappeared, a familiar warm current streaming electric through my entire body.

"Welcome to Tlalocan," the old painter said with a warm smile.

"What better Heaven could there be?" I responded, "What's the movie about?"

"You."

"Me?"

What better place to watch your life flash by before your eyes? What better view than from Tlalocan on a movie screen? You got to see your whole life story from the best seat in Heaven's house, the back row.

"Tlalocan is a Heaven for heroes and warriors." I said, "why am I here?"

"Pep," the old painter laughed as his face dissolved into a cluster of dark blue storm clouds that overlook the entire big screen, "you are both hero and warrior. You've been fighting the ghosts of your own insecurities, guilt and fears all your life. You are a Warrior. A Ghost Warrior."

I would hear that name again shortly in a nearby zapateria where the true identity of my guardian angel, this old painter who seemed so very familiar to me since my arrival on the Boulevard of the Dead, would be revealed. In this revelation, there would be great healing as the largest piece of my fractured soul would finally be restored.

In old fashioned Senseround, lightning struck and thunder rolled as the title of the film appeared against the dark blue clouds. The title, stretching out across the massive IMAX screen in glittering electric blue lettering;

The View from Tlalocan

From the back row, I watched my whole life flash before my eyes. Among the flashing collage of scenes I relived on the big screen:

The death bed scene of a high priest of the court of Pakal in the Pre-Colombian Mayan city of Palenque, a jade jaguar nagual leading my spirit into a white light.

FLASH

A fast-forwarded blur of various lives lived and white lights. All tales I am aching to share someday but not here.

FLASH

My birth in a Mexico City hospital, the transparent figures of the old painter and the jade jaguar watching over the blessed event from a darkened corner of the room.

FLASH

Myself, one year later, being treated by Dr. Luis, for severe dehydration. Dr. Luis, who chose heroically not to drive with his brothers to Guadalajara to watch a soccer game so that he could stay and save my life and whose brothers died on their way. It was this good doctor who came to believe that I saved his life as he saved mine. Feverish and delirious, baby Pep looked past the doctor's shoulder at the old painter, who comforted him with a lullaby that no one else in the room could hear.

FLASH

The nightly fights between my mother and father. A little boy, afraid of the dark and the unknown, hearing his daddy cry, "I'm old, I'm old, I'm going to die" and "you're going to leave me because I'm old."

FLASH

The nights I was visited by the old painter and the jade jaguar, turning towards the wall so as to ignore them and, a few years later, turning on the television to fill my head with the necessary noise that would block them out completely.

FLASH

My parent's divorce, my sister and I crying as we heard the news, crying as we waved goodbye to my father, leaving him behind, alone at 69, waving goodbye from the back seat of a Chevy Nova, his frail form shrinking into the distance until we couldn't see him.

FLASH

That night at the dinner table with Horace and my mother when I stated, "when I grow up, I'm going to be a high school basketball coach like Ken Howard in "The White Shadow."

FLASH

The trauma of high school, Chris Driscoll, the fight on the bus, being cut from the basketball team my first year, my year long bout with hepatitis, graduating college, becoming a teacher, and running away from the theater and my acting dreams.

FLASH

My first day as a teacher, a young man dressed to impress in a collar and a tie, turning nervously away from a chalkboard to face a spirited class of middle schoolers, then amazed at how easily I got them to settle down.

"Excuse me," I spoke sternly, "Sit."

They sat. Looking at the clock I saw that I had over 45 minutes left of class. Having heard horror stories about how difficult it was to manage a class, I was surprised when my students did exactly as I had instructed. I never dreamed it would be so easy.

It's not. You were born for it. A born teacher.

FLASH

I saw myself with the soul mate, the girl I should have stuck with but let get away, at the steps of a local elementary school where, beneath a full orange moon, we had a picnic on our first date.

Actually, you closed your eyes through this part.

FLASH

The joy that came with the news that I was soon to be a father and the subsequent births of my children.

FLASH

The days I visited my father as Alzheimer's ate away at him. The days I didn't visit because I didn't want to see my father so diminished.

FLASH

The passing of my father, how he would come to me at a Lake Tahoe campground in the middle of the night to let me know that he was dying and to say, "goodbye."

FLASH

The many fights with my wife and the unhappiness of my marriage.

FLASH

Finally, an aerial view of the fatal accident itself, high above the intersection of Beach and Main, paramedics cutting through my wrecked Honda with the Jaws of Life.

The whole film zipped by in a blur but not without overwhelming me with the sense that I had just sat through a four-hour epic by DeMille. With every scene, with each flashing recollection came a warm rush as I felt lost and fragmented parts of my soul return to me.

Death at an early age, such as dying in a seemingly random car accident at 35...

It wasn't so random.

...never seems to make sense to anyone. Yet, everything in my *View from Tlalocan*, including my death, seemed to make perfect sense. It all added up. I was on a collision course with that gray van since I was born. When the film was over, the last dark frame did not read "The End" but instead;

"A New Beginning."

A BASKETBALL COURT

I have many passions.

Today, reborn a Ghost Warrior; a teacher, healer, storyteller and basketball coach, I believe that all my artistic, athletic and spiritual inclinations have come together in a magical way to inspire and enlighten those who have lost hope for their dreams.

They make up the many brushes you use to paint the world blue.

Just as my life made more sense with *The View from Tlalocan*, so too had the purpose behind each of my gifts become revealed to me. As you know, however, before my life-ending, life-changing collision, nothing really seemed to make sense in my life at all. You might recall that prior to my journey down this Boulevard the Dead, I was desperate and out of control.

As a kid, I was horribly and quietly troubled by the spectral voices and the angry growl of a large cat that haunted me from the dark shadows of my bedroom at night. Also, while I was able to hide the surreal angst caused by my parent's divorce, I was emotionally paralyzed by the thoughts of my poor father, wasting away with age and Alzheimer's - Cassandra, his new wife, sticking valiantly but alone by his side - while I now lived a privileged life in Westlake Village with my mother and Horace. I sought escape from this unbearable guilt in my bedroom and a little basketball court at the local elementary school.

As a teenager, basketball was my life. It became everything to me. I was fourteen when my mother walked me into my first basketball camp on the campus of Cal State University, Northridge. That's a little old to be introduced to a sport but I fell in love with basketball the instant I walked into the gym, the second my fingertips touched the leather ball.

From that moment on, basketball became my ultimate passion, absorbing every aspect of my life. Unlike, the arts, which seemed to keep my head in the clouds, basketball kept my feet firmly on the ground. For me, basketball was no less an art than drawing, but it was physical and concrete. From 14 on, I spent 4 or 5 hours each day, still alone, practicing at game speed with every dribble, ankle-breaking cross-over and shot ever conceived by man. I'm sure, also, that I must have created a few new moves as well – all of which I later taught to my own son and which helped him to become a high school basketball star.

Henrietta

Henrietta was my basketball. Again, I was introduced to Henrietta and to basketball rather late as a kid but once I found her, it was love at first sight. Now I was thoroughly obsessed with basketball. I practiced with Henrietta every day, hours and hours, at the local elementary school, on the street, in my backyard and, when my mother was away, even, rearranging furniture, in the house. At night, I slept with Henrietta as a young boy would cuddle up with a teddy bear and in the morning I would sneak outside to do ball handling drills before breakfast.

It was poetic to find Henrietta on that altar in the panaderia, alongside pictures of others who had passed away, long after she made her way to the basketball graveyard. She had quite an impact on me and meant so much to me as a kid. Like all-night movies, comics and drawing, Henrietta may have indeed helped to save my life.

The place I would go to practice was a little basketball court on the small campus of Westlake Elementary School. Rather than head out to the park, I chose to practice alone on this little court, where I could practice at my own pace (which was consistently furious) and, in this privacy, still be able to live my life in my head.

Living life in my head as I did, and still do, allowed my imagination to run wild. In my imagination, I wasn't playing alone but going hard against any number of fierce NBA legends who pushed me to my limits.

It is a great testament to the power of visualization that, when I did compete against others, my speed and skill allowed me to dominate.

Since we were no longer living in the San Fernando Valley but in Westlake now, the La Reina was no longer an option for me to escape to when times got tough. Now, if I wasn't locked up in my bedroom, drawing and watching television, I was at Westlake Elementary, practicing basketball and running away from all my guilty anguish.

Many know of my intense passion for basketball and I am well known and respected as a coach and mentor in my area. It might surprise most to discover that I never played basketball in my senior year of high school. I quit.

You travelled to Europe that summer, knowing that you would not play basketball when you returned...

...and played soccer...

A sport you never liked or were never particularly good at.

Soccer, a sport I didn't like then and find myself still bored to tears by today.

Unless it's the World Cup. Then, it gets interesting.

My basketball prime was spent in parks all over Los Angeles and the San Fernando Valley.

My nature was fragile at the time. I could not stand up to all the Chris Driscolls that made my life such a living hell in high school. I decided to disappear into an invisible sport and soccer, in the seventies, was as invisible as a high school sport could get in a white, upper middle-class environment. Soccer was also a sport where my brown skin generated grand expectations of me. It was assumed that because I was Mexican that I would be good and that I would excel. To both my teammates' and coach's chagrin, however, I wasn't very good. We thought you'd be better, the coaches and players would often say.

Nevertheless, basketball and coaching were and still are two of my great passions. I coached my first park and recreation team when I was 15 and kept coaching young kids through my college years and into my twenties. I became a high school varsity basketball coach at 32, winning a league championship in my second year. Now, five teams later, in my 50's, my passion for everything basketball burns as hot as it did when I first discovered the sport at 14.

In many ways, I believe that basketball saved my life, keeping me from hurting myself and, while I got myself into several sick and sticky messes, kept me out of any more trouble than I had already created for myself. Though I have no college or NBA tales to tell, basketball meant no less to me than it did to Jordan or Magic. To basketball I gave my heart and soul. As the dance was to my father, basketball is to me. It is a dance.

Whether as a street player or as a career coach, I still find much purpose in my passion for this sport and in teaching the importance of discipline and practice. In basketball, I have connected somehow with the Quetzal. If it is true, and I have full faith that it is, that in our passion we find our purpose, then I have found great moments of true fulfillment as a basketball coach and as the shaman of my own Ghost Warrior B'Ball Dojo. A friend and coaching colleague once confided to me that, "Outside of being called, Daddy, there is nothing better than being called, Coach." In this, I can fully relate.

Again, I found myself on the Boulevard of the Dead, looking now at my 15 year old self practicing like a mad man on the small basketball court at Westlake Elementary School. I smiled nostalgically at the sight of the bright red warm up suit I was wearing. That suit was a Christmas gift. I think I wore that suit for a straight week, to school and to bed, before I switched back to jeans, polos and pajamas.

Observing the practice from a drinking fountain, I saw the old painter, my jade jaguar napping at his feet. He tipped his cap and gave me a nod before sipping from a weak stream of water.

As I watched my younger self plow through a series of Pistol Pete's, which is a name applied to ball handling drills perfected by the great Pete Maravich, I noticed that tears were streaming down the boy's face. This was the day I learned my father had locked himself in a bathroom, pledging never to come out unless his boy came to visit him. By this time, Alzheimer's had already taken an early grip on my father; his brilliant mind was slipping and he was scared.

"Cassandra called," my mother told me that same morning, "she says that your father is crying and begging to see you. He's locked himself in the bathroom and he's calling for you."

I did not go to him. I was too afraid, too afraid to deal with mortality and the deterioration of my hero.

I told you to go to your father.

I didn't hear you.

Your highest self nevertheless knew to go.

Yes, it did.

Watching myself practice, I realized that I had left behind a huge chunk of my soul on this small court, as I had at the La Reina and in high school. There I was, in all my guilt and pain, practicing, sweating, living in my head, imagining that I was going one on one against Jerry West with thirty seconds on the clock, trying to wish away all the pain with every shot I took. It didn't work, never did, and I carried the guilt of that day with me, along with the greater guilt of not being there for my father when he died, until the day of my own death at that fog shrouded intersection on the Boulevard of the Dead.

"Tell him that it's okay," the old painter directed me telepathically.

The boy shot the ball, elbow in with a beautiful follow through, swishing it through a metal chain net. Hitting the ground, the ball bounced towards me and I caught it. The boy approached me, looking to retrieve the ball. At first, he stared quizzical, looking at me with much of the same puzzlement that must have crossed my own face when I first laid eyes upon the old painter. He recognized me, but he didn't know from where. It took less than a moment though before he knew who I was. He walked up to me and we stood at the sideline staring at each other, tears now running from both our eyes.

"Tell him," I heard the old painter repeat with a soft whisper in my head.

"It's okay," I told the boy. I told myself.

Wiping away tears, the boy reached out to me. At first, I thought he wanted to embrace me.

"Henrietta's coming with me," he said.

The boy snatched the ball from my hands, smiled then disappeared into thin air.

My jaguar yawned, and I felt a warm rush.

TIA MARIA SOUP

Through a dense gray-black fog I was able to make out a long black driveway that led to the sketchy outline of a small Victorian home. Behind me I heard the snarl of my jaguar as invisible paws nudged at my back, pushing me forward through the fog and toward the house.

As I proceeded up the driveway, the fog receded. Memories returned, and I was now able to discern where I was. It was my Tia Maria's house. An old Ford Falcon was parked at the end of the driveway by a red tiled porch. That was my father's car.

As a young boy, my father took me often to the home of his sister, my Tia Maria and her husband, Tio Tony. Until this moment, though, I hadn't thought much about either of them. Tio Tony was a quiet silver haired old man with a joyful countenance, who, every time I remember seeing him, whittled away at a chunk of wood with a small pocket knife. He was a descendent of the De La Osa family, original settlers of the San Fernando Valley, whose homes are preserved as historic landmarks at the Rancho Encinos Park in Encino, California.

Tia Maria, as I remember her, was a petite woman with dark indigenous features, glasses, a big smile and a raspy voice who was always in the kitchen. What I remember most about my Tia was the soup that she made which, along with a warm pot of beans was always simmering on her stove. It was a seemingly simple fideo, as might be found in many Latino homes; a light tomato-based broth with thin noodles and boiled chicken. To my sister and I, though, this soup was a magical brew. We just couldn't get enough of Tia Maria's Soup. For years after my parent's divorce, I celebrated my birthday with Tia Maria's Soup, my mother's own delicious version of it.

As I neared the porch, Tio Tony stepped out through a screen door to greet me. He took a seat on a swing chair and began to whittle at a piece of wood

"Pasale," he said, inviting me to enter the house, "pasale."

The house was dark except for the light that came from the kitchen down the hall. Already I could smell her soup. As I feel my father's presence in the aroma of the picadillo he would cook, it is in the smell of her sopa that my Tia's essence still lives.

I sensed my jaguar nearby as I made my way down the dark hall, following my nose to the kitchen. Although it was dark, I could still make out old photographs on the wall, Victorian pictures of my grandparents and, interestingly, drawings that looked to be of Native American design. One, in particular, of a jaguar shape-shifting into a warrior atop a desert mesa surrounded by desperate Native American spirits begging, I figured, to be healed.

I entered the kitchen to find Tia Maria at the stove, stirring her soup. Above her stove, a picture of the Virgin Mary hung from the wall. My Tia was barefoot and wearing a white huipil. She was so small that she had to stand on her toes to get her wooden ladle over the big pot to stir. At first, her back to me, I didn't think she knew I was there. But, like Julia, she knew.

"Pasale," she said, inviting me into the kitchen and, her back to me still, pointing to the table where I saw only one table setting.

"Sientate," she continued. Laying down the ladle, she then reached for a smoking tye of white sage. As I took my seat, I watched Tia Maria smudge the air around the steaming pot of fideo and whisper a prayer in a language I had never heard before. At first, I assumed it was Spanish but as I listened more carefully it sounded closer to the Native American prayers sung by the Medicine Man and other esteemed medicine men and shamans I heard sing in Tucson several years before I died.

They were Tarahumara prayers she sung.

Setting the burning sage onto a small plate, she picked up the ladle, reached for a bowl and filled it with soup. With a big smile, she turned around to greet me. She resembled Julia, as Julia may have appeared if arthritis had not warped her body and twisted her features, if blindness had not robbed her of the light in her eyes.

Tia Maria was old, yes, her face withered, and what was left of her teeth had yellowed. Nevertheless, there was a youthful energy, a timeless jubilance that radiated from her big brown eyes and her smile as she approached me.

"You know what day this is, don't you?" she asked as she served me some soup. In life, Tia Maria spoke to me in Spanish only but here she spoke in English.

Steam rose from the bowl, the rich aroma of fideo warming my nostrils, calming my thoughts and instantly transporting me into an altered state.

"October first," she continued.

"The day I died," I whispered blissfully, high off the intoxicating fumes of Tia Maria's soup. Sipping a spoonful of fideo, the hot soup warmed my innards with the same electric rush I felt upon recovering pieces of myself along the Boulevard of the Dead. Eating Tia Maria soup was a soul-retrieval in itself. In an instant, a rush of childhood memories inundated my thoughts, of forgotten happy times with my father; playing catch at the beach, his bedtime stories, his hearty wonderful laugh and those times when he would look proudly at me to say, "My boy."

"This is a special day. It is the day you were born again, your re-birth day. It is also the Yaqui Day of the Dead. It is now that the borders between the worlds of the living and the dead merge. It is no mistake that your jaguar led you here on this day to cross over and mingle with the departed and recover fragments of your shattered soul."

We heard an urgent knock at the back door. Tia Maria peered over her shoulder through a window over the sink and sighed with exasperation.

"No rest," she groaned, then turned to me again, "no rest for the curandera." *It is as the Medicine Man told you, "the only reward for service is more service."*

Through the window, I saw from where I sat that there were people lining up outside her kitchen. Some of these people had their faces pressed desperately against the glass attempting to get a look inside. Many of them looked to be covered by a black tar-like substance.

"Who are they?" I asked.

Just then, the face of a grotesquely scarred woman appeared at the window, her scorched cheeks bleeding. In life, that face might have repulsed me more but here, in Tia Maria's kitchen, I felt only compassion for the poor souls lined up outside.

"They are hungry," Tia Maria answered.

Lifting the bowl to my lips, I drank down the rest of the soup.

"The soup is delicious," I said, "I can see why they stand in line."

Her soup was brewed and conceived in the kitchen of the Quetzal. She took no credit for it. She was only there to serve. It was more than just soup they hungered for. It was healing. It was not their bellies they sought to fill but their souls. It was God they sought.

Peeking out the window, she counted the numbers in line, her gaze extending to the end of the long driveway and even deeper into the fog.

"There's a lot of them today, more than usual," she snickered, "but, then, it is a holiday."

As a child, I paid no attention, but now, here, I was beginning to remember that there were always people lined up outside Tia Maria's house when we came to visit. Several years after my eventual return to the Land of the Living, it would come as no surprise to me when Cassandra told me, on a Father's Day many years down the road, that my Tia Maria was a Tarahumara medicine woman, a curandera, and that she was well known for her healing ways.

She opened a cupboard and brought down a stack of ceramic bowls with Mayan designs. The door opened by itself as one grizzled old guy stood at the front of the line, waiting to be served. Tia Maria placed a steaming bowl of soup into his outstretched tar covered hands.

"Gracias, senora," the old grizzled guy said, bowing his head, then turning to make room for the next in line. One by one Tia Maria served her soup from a pot that never seemed to diminish.

"They are refugees," Tia Maria explained, serving one bowl of soup after another, poor soul after poor soul, "from the river."

The River of the Damned. They were there to escape the illusion of the Man in Black and the lie that they immersed themselves in their whole lives. They wanted to be whole again.

The next person in line was drenched by this thick black goo. It was as if he had been dipped in melted dark chocolate. Looking through the door at the long line outside, I saw that there were a million others covered by the same black slime.

They escaped before their souls could be harvested by the Man in Black and lost for eternity. Something, whatever it was I cannot say, opened their hearts to the Quetzal and to hear God calling out to them just in time. In that they were saved. They were led to your Tia to get right before returning to Heaven. Some had lost themselves so deeply in the illusion they had no idea who they were anymore. This soup helped them remember and induced within them the same warm rush of soul retrieval that you experienced along your journey down the Boulevard of the Dead.

"Here," she said, placing a bowl in my hands, "help me serve."

One at a time they came, one desperately lost soul after another, hands outstretched, reaching gratefully for Tia Maria's Soup. Outside, the fog cleared as each person who drank the soup and was healed radiated a glowing warmth that melted away the oppressive dark mists. Amazingly, I felt that familiar warm rush within me each time one of these souls was healed at my Tia's back doorstep.

Several times, while we were serving soup, I looked at my Tia to behold a wondrous transformation. One moment, she was my old and nearly toothless Tia Maria, the next she was as the Virgin Mary, La Virgen de Guadalupe, a blazing aura of white light encircling her. It was in one of those moments that she smiled at me and said, "He is proud."

As the last of the hopeless lined up at the back door, Tio Tony shuffled into the kitchen, still whittling at a piece of wood which was just now beginning to take form.I tried to get a look at what it was that he carved but he carefully concealed his masterwork with his pudgy liver spotted hands.

"Es tiempo," he said, "time to go."

Tia Maria nodded farewell as she served the last few and I walked out with my Tio, passing again through the dark hallway towards the front door. Tio Tony opened thedoor and I could see that all the fog had now cleared around the old house. Sun was shining brightly onto the porch as I stepped outside and I noticed immediately that my father's Falcon was no longer there.

"Was my father here? I saw his old Falcon here when I arrived," I asked Tio Tony.

"Si," Tio Tony nodded, "he was here earlier for sopa. He's fine now."

"I was hoping that I might have seen him."

"En tiempo. En tiempo.".

The sun hit me hard as I stepped onto the driveway and with that I was overcomeby pulsating waves of warm energy that again streamed through my entire being. It ws as if millions of lost Pep soul fragments had instantly been returned to me. That high, however, was fleeting. While I did experience in that moment a greater sense of what I can only describe as completeness, there was nevertheless something missing. I was not yet truly whole.

When one truly becomes whole again, we all become whole again. We are all one.

I saw the old painter now, a jade jaguar at his side, waiting for me at the end of the driveway. As I made my way toward him, Tio Tony tapped my shoulder.

"Wait," he said, extending his hands to me.

I was surprised to find a wooded jaguar in his hands.

"Don't forget your nagual."

A LITTLE OLD LADY AT THE CORNER

On the foggy corner of Beach and Main, I saw the specter of a little old lady in a gray flannel coat and laced shawl. She stood almost like a flickering transparent flame between the very cement lamp post and Latino music store where, in The Land of the Living, my car ended up in a smashed-up heap.

Hearing me behind her, she turned, her whole form becoming solid now so that I could no longer see through her. She walked up to me with a vacant and hopeless stare.

"Have you seen my father?" she asked with a quivering voice.

This was a woman I remembered from my childhood, an old lady I treated very badly one day. I didn't even know her name.

While I spent most of my time in my bedroom and in my head, there were always plenty of kids about the pool or hanging out by the parking area if I ever wanted to go out and play at the old Del Valle Apartments.

On one such rare summer day when I decided to venture from my dark bedroom into the light of day, I was wrestling with my friends at the main entrance of our apartment building. Finding myself in an inescapable headlock, I spotted an old lady making her way up the sidewalk. She was the crazy lady we all made fun of, the sad nut who knocked on each of our doors every week or so to ask, "Have you seen my father?"

Seeing her approach, I tapped out and my friend released me from his iron hold. I got quickly to my feet and ran to meet the old lady as she approached the steps leading into the lobby. She was a weird curiosity to us and a target to be teased.

"Have you seen my father?" she asked us, "he told me to wait for him and he never came back."

We were so sinfully wrong to taunt that sad little old lady the way we did. It was more than being juvenile; it was inexcusable at any age. We were horrible to be so insensitive and cruel to this poor lost soul but I soon took that nastiness to a whole different level.

To this day, I don't know what meanness or nasty impulse got into me that day. Surely, the anger building within me over my parent's divorce can be no excuse, but for some reason, the demon in me thought it would be funny to come up from behind this little old lady and push her.

I felt her fragility the instant my palms pushed against her bony back and I was ashamed the moment her sharp knees hit the sidewalk. I knew instantly that I had sinned. Instead of laughs there were shrieks of shock. My friends were horrified and from far away I heard the mother of my best friend scream out from her upstairs window.

There was a commotion afterwards that I'll never forget, and a spanking that still stings. As is my way, though, there could be no flogging more brutal than that which I imposed upon myself. My guilt has always been my greatest punishment. It was more than a month before I would venture out from my bedroom again.

I am guilty of many shameful things in my life, which have weighed heavily on my conscience, things I have sworn to atone for. If, today, there is a daily effort on my part to be pure and impeccable in my intent and my action, it is not because I am holier than thou. This effort at impeccability derives from my own ascent from darkness, my renewed commitment to living in the moment, my faith in my new awareness and hope for a new beginning.

While I was only ten at the time, the shame I felt for pushing that little old lady haunted me into adulthood. It was difficult for a while to reconcile my horrid action with what I always tried to tell myself; you're a good person, Pep. Good people, even kids just don't push little old ladies to the ground.

Now before me on the Boulevard of the Dead, the little old lady lifted her frail hand, and pointed at an old zapateria, a quaint little shoe store, across the fog swamped boulevard. Around its dark corner I could see the tail-end of an old Ford Falcon. Through a tinted window I saw movement, a lean dark silhouette making its way to the entrance and disappearing behind the wall. Then, with a creak, the front door opened slightly.

I turned to see the little old lady back at the corner, a shaft of brilliant white light streaking down through the thick fog behind her. With a smile, she stepped into the light and slowly dematerialized within it. Then, as if God flicked the "off" switch, the shaft of light disappeared.

"Father," I heard the old lady whisper from somewhere in Heaven. With this I felt another warm rush.

Another loud creak from across the boulevard had me turn my head again toward the old zapateria where the door was now opened wide. On this ethereal street where everything was a sign, I saw this as an obvious invitation to enter.

A ZAPATERIA

Tarilla, Tarilla, Tarilla, Crash pa!

I walked through the open door into the old zapateria, this little shoe store at the last corner of the Boulevard of the Dead, the last stop before heading out of town and into a bright white mist. I assumed that white mist to be Heaven. It was the soft light from this mist, streaking through half closed blinds that brought a muted glow to everything in the shop.

The smell of leather was thick about the store and all variety of dance boots and shoes were displayed along the walls and at the windows. On the counter, by the register, stood a miniature castle tower made of plaster, the very same one that Cassandra gave to me during our hike the summer before.

Somewhere within the zapateria, the jaguar growled and I found myself reaching into my pocket where I kept Tio Tony's wood carved gift, my jaguar. I was nervous when I entered this shop but now, clutching the wooden jaguar tightly, I was emboldened to venture deeper into the murkily lit shop.

As I approached the counter, I noticed that there was someone else in the dingy shop with me, someone beyond the counter rummaging around a darkened stockroom. Squinting, I could barely discern the hunched back of an old man. The fact that he was dressed in black from head to toe made it even more difficult to make him out, but he was there like a ghost haunting the place. As the door swung shut behind me, he straightened up and turned to greet me. At first, his face still in shadow, I didn't recognize him.

"Someday, you will be all grown up and you will be approached by an old man. He will say to you, 'Pep, Pep, don't you remember me?' You will look at him and say, 'I'm sorry, sir, but I don't know who you are."

"Pep," he asked, "don't you know me?"

The voice was familiar but the face still indistinct in the darkness. A weak shaft of white light did, however, illumine in his hands a pair of black ebony castanets that he was polishing with fine grained sandpaper.

"Who are you?" I asked.

The dark figure stepped into the light and I saw that it was my father. Just as he had once predicted, there would come a time when I wouldn't know him. As he approached me, his fingers began rapping the edges of the castanets and he whispered, "tarilla, tarilla, tarilla, crash- pa."

I would have embraced him immediately if not for a certain disbelief and an avalanche of guilt that seemed to straitjacket me and hold me in check at a distance.

Forgetting my Father

I've spoken of the guilt that crippled me upon my father's passing. My father did not simply predict that I would have difficulty recognizing him as he got older, but that I would forget him altogether, that his son would someday deny him and leave him alone. Shamefully, I did. If not for Cassandra, I don't know what would have become of him. He might have been abandoned by the world.

Cassandra was my father's fourth and last wife. While they were separated by forty years, she loved my father, took care of him through illness, Alzheimer's and his own car accident, stood by him through his convalescence and was there for him when his boy was not. When his time finally came, his last breath was taken with his head on her lap, lying beneath a lemon tree in a garden of roses and Serrano peppers.

While he wasn't technically alone, while he was loved and taken care of by Cassandra, I knew in my heart how badly it hurt him that I wasn't there for him, that his boy had abandoned him. Only now, as a father myself, can I fully comprehend the pain that he must have suffered at losing his children to divorce, then at wasting away without even his son beside him.

Hard to forget that still Sunday morning, years before when I was just nine, sitting on my father's lap by the window, a dove cooing outside, my sister on my mother's knee.

"Your daddy and I are not going to be living together anymore," my mother gently broke the news.

I've heard much talk about the resiliency of kids and how they recover and adapt quickly to divorce. For me, these are the flimsy rationales of parents who hope to discard their own accountability. Far be it from me to suggest that people should never get divorced. If the marriage is bad, then get out.

You've lived through some bad marriages.

I'm not proud. Still, life is about learning and who should be punished by imprisoning themselves to a life of unhappiness? No one. But, let us not fool ourselves, the scars of divorce run deep and last a lifetime on our children.

Your own children should know.

How does any child recover from a broken home, at watching a daddy break down and cry, or from that last wave good-bye? As an old man, despite all the soul retrieval, one shard of my soul still hides out somewhere in limbo. I still feel the pain of watching my daddy cry.

As a child, my mother never physically kept me from my father and we didn't move that far away, a matter of a couple miles, no more. So, why didn't I see my father more? One reason was the dust.

My father was an animal lover of the highest order. There must have been more than six cats in that home, two dogs and a cage full of canaries.

Cassandra loved animals, too. A month didn't go by where she didn't find a stray cat or injured bird to save. It was her calling, I believe, to save animals and, as with me many years later, people, too.

At times their home seemed like an animal rescue center where animals of every kind seemed to show up by instinct, or maybe even by some strange word of mouth within the animal kingdom, to their doorstep and once there, live harmoniously, even the most primordial of enemies, among themselves.

Like my father, I had terrible allergies and the dust in his home, together with the shedding of cat and dog hair, triggered horrible allergic episodes characterized by wheezing, rapid-fire sneezing, hives and eyes swollen shut. To this day, wherever I may visit, it takes less than one strand of cat hair to prompt a flare-up. It was more than just the animals about the house that initiated my allergies, though. It was, as I have said already, the dust.

No longer living a life on the stage, my father spent every day in his garage where he fashioned his own castanets out of ebony and mahogany. His garage was equipped with all the essential tools and machines for woodwork and my father made good and constant use of it all.

My father wasn't just a dancer, he was a master artist. A creator. That garage was his dojo, his refuge from time and reality, his place of retreat, his magical little world of creation. And, boy, did he create. A multitude of the most exquisite castanets found form there and when they were done and polished, my father would test them for tone and precision, walking about the garage or even the hall and den of our home."Tarilla, tarilla, tarilla, crash pa." Keeping his fingers sharp and nimble, he rapped the smooth, dark wood surfaces to the repeating rhythm of "tarilla, tarilla, tarilla, crash pa."

More than just castanets, my father's den of creation churned out cupboards, benches, crucifixes, a sports car for my Pinewood Derby event and, his most brilliant creation, a masterfully scaled yet ultimately doomed plaster castle.

All this creation led to a lot of dust. Dust was everywhere, not just in the garage but all about the house, and upon my father as well. He brought the dust from the garage with him into the house. For me, to hug my father was to sneeze.

In this house, dust built upon dust upon animal hairs and more dust. It was everywhere; on the counters, the furniture and my bedcovers. Certainly, my father was a master artist, a sorcerer with words, wood and dance. He was, however, like me, more preoccupied with his art than with housework. That's not to say he lacked hygiene. My father was very clean, and his house was clean and in order – just very, very dusty.

To some degree I blamed my allergies. Because of them, weekends at my father's home was miserable and nearly un-survivable. My allergies were much more severe than my father's. For him it was enough to carry about a nasal spray he called, a whiffler. Two sprays here and there during the day and two at bedtime – he was fine. My sister, also, seemed unaffected by the dust and the animals and even owns several dogs today. By Sunday night, when my mother would come to pick us up, I was a swollen, mucus heaving, sneezing and wheezing mess. For me, coming home to my mother's dust free two-bedroom apartment, the solitude of my own room, my black and white television and the smell of lemon Pledge was a lifesaver.

It wasn't just the dust and the animals that kept me away, though. There was more.

If there is romance in the manner I view my life, a habit to glorify and, as my friends have observed, see life bigger than it is: to feel God's caress in a breeze, to sense the beginning, middle and end of each minute, to wonder what it is the babbling brook might be saying to me, if my head really is on most occasions in the clouds, then it is from my father that this has been passed down. This romance, this way of seeing life is but one of the hereditary traits I love most about myself and it is this romance that makes me feel close to my father so long after his passing.

My father, as Horace would also become, was my hero. In his glory days as a dancer, he met and worked with many of the talented stars of Hollywood's Golden Era. I was mesmerized by the stories he would tell me of his friendships and encounters with screen idols like Orson Welles, Fred Astaire, Rita Hayworth, Ramon Navarro and others. I would lie on my bed for hours, leaving through the pages of his old scrapbooks, staring at black and white photos of him in costume, seeing his name in headlines, reading about him in old articles and reviews of his shows. He was a magnificent storyteller and loved to perform, whether on stage before 20,000 at the Hollywood Bowl or at the dinner table in front of a dozen or so guests. These are the things I look back on most fondly, remembering my father in this way; a passionate artist, a wonderful storyteller with a hearty laugh.

On occasion, my father shared with me memories of his own encounters with strange voices and visions as a child. For him, though, there was no old painter whispering in the darkness, and no jade jaguars. **He had his own angels.**

He was haunted by a strange green face that would materialize on his bedroom wall, recurring dreams of a past life as a Mayan High Priest and sometimes a beautiful spectral dancer.

He saw this dancer even as an old man, and Cassandra saw her too. One night, Cassandra woke up to see a beautiful flamenco dancer floating horizontally above my father, beckoning to him. Cassandra was horrified, not necessarily by the specter but by the sight of my father, mesmerized, reaching out to it. For a moment, she thought she was going to lose him, that my father would depart with this dancing angel.

Whoever this spectral dancer may have been, whether angel or the ghost of a former love betrayed at the hour of death in a past life by my father, or whatever this green face my father saw as a child represented, whatever their messages, my father never told me. Maybe, he, himself, never knew. I have a feeling that he avoided these specters all his life, that he was afraid of them, just as I feared the old painter and my jaguar nagual.

The Cenote

Cassandra believed that the ghosts my father dreaded most were from a past life. Cassandra shared with me a story of my father that I had never heard before. A tale that was to answer many questions about my father and about what I would later come to know as our shamanic bond. It would seem that both my father and I were Mayan High Priests in past lives.

Cassandra recounted my father's recurring and most disturbing dream. In his lucid dream, my father was a Mayan High Priest who was involved in the ritual sacrifice of a beautiful Mayan virgin. In his dream it was his duty as a priest to throw the young woman into the cenote, a massive limestone cavity in the ground (possibly in the Mayan city of Uxmal) where she would be sucked up by the water below as an offering to the gods.

The problem was that my father and this sacrificial lamb were already secret lovers. Together they made a plan. It would be impossible for the woman to escape death but together they committed to a lover's death pact. If she were to die so too would he. As soon as he pushed her into the mouth of the cenote, it was agreed, my father would also take the fatal plunge so that they would face eternity and the wrath of the gods together.

When the ritual of sacrifice arrived, my father did as was expected and pushed his love into the cenote. Worshippers cheered as her body plummeted into the waters below, where she was immediately swallowed up by the strong currents and lost forever in the labyrinth of underwater caverns beneath their feet. In that moment of truth, however, my father froze as he would also freeze several lifetimes later at the time of his own mother's passing. He feared death too much to jump and she died alone.

It was a dream my father regarded more as a memory from a past life, one he claimed to have dreamed over and over since his childhood. Because of this memory, my father was haunted by remorse over many lifetimes. The name of this ghost was guilt. It was this shame over his cowardice and his betrayal that made him feel unworthy of anyone's love. Is it any wonder that my father was married four times? As famous and brilliant as my father was, he never felt worthy of being loved. As with me, guilt was the illusion's unrelenting champion over my father and it poisoned him.

★ ★

It was in our blood to see things. This is why my father never dismissed my reports of strange voices, shadows on the wall and a jaguar's growl. This is why, whenever I spoke to him about my fears, he would simply run his hand over the back of my head and say, "I know." That was enough for me to know that I wasn't crazy and all that I had been experiencing - seeing, hearing and dreaming - was real. Of course, these small comforts didn't change anything. I still wished these visions gone.

My father couldn't help that he was old, or, that as an artist, he lived life in his own head, detached from everyone else's reality, lost in his own romantic world. He spent most of his time teaching flamenco dancing in his living room, stealing my GI-Joe action figures to demonstrate proper dance form, or in his garage, making castanets and plaster castles. By nightfall, he was drained and sitting down in front of the television, watching *Ed Sullivan*, *Star Trek* and *Bonanza*, before passing out in his chair. Many times, I would wake up to find my father asleep, an old test signal on the television screen.

He was old and my mother's new boyfriend, who was to become my stepfather and my new hero, was young. Horace was twenty-six years old, a cross between Robert Redford and Brad Pitt with sandy blond hair, a tanned six-pack and a cool white VW bug he bought for a hundred bucks. With Horace, I could wrestle like a maniac, play air hockey and shoot hoops. These were things that I never did with my father.

On Friday afternoons, when Horace came courting my mother for the weekend, he'd bring my sister and I a bag full of candies and gum that we'd devour before dinner. He captured our hearts with candy. Saturday and Sunday mornings were spent watching old westerns and Universal horrors. It was Horace who exposed me to classic movies and to literature. Through him I was introduced to great filmmakers; Hitchcock, Ford, Hemingway and to my favorite writer, Charles Dickens. Even today, my top favorite movies of all time are ones he introduced me to at nine-years-old and it's because of him that *A Christmas Carol* is my favorite story.

My mother never kept me from my father. Still, I felt somehow that by loving my father, I wasn't loving my mother or, even, that I was being disloyal to Horace. I'm sure it's common within the dynamics of broken homes that parents might put other parents down. In my home, my mother said unflattering things about my father, how he didn't care or how he doesn't pay dime one.

When I divorced my own wife many years later, I was guilty of cracking and my ugliest side emerged as I leveled horribly disparaging rants against the mother of my children. It is one of my great crimes against my own children that I spoke so ill of their mother. Anger is such a poison. No matter her efforts to completely destroy my life, I should never have sunk so low to have said the things I did. My purging only hurt my children more.

To my father's credit, he never said anything negative about my mother. Indeed, I don't think I ever heard my father utter a nasty word about anyone. It was quite the opposite as he was always sure to let me know what a beautiful woman my mother was and always adamant that I never say the word hate.

My mother and Horace were, of course, wonderful parents. There are no villains in a divorce, I believe, just people who are hurting within the context of the Man in Black's illusion and that hurt finds many expressions.

Between the allergies, a younger hero and a fear of death, I chose my mother. I had this unshakable fear that one morning I would wake up and my father would be dead, and I didn't want to be there when he died. Plus, thinking about him dying got me thinking about me dying.

These morbid thoughts often came to me at night, in my bed, looking up from my covers through the window at the millions of stars in the blackened sky. I would wonder about the universe, about where it began and where it ended. Is there a wall where the universe ends and does another universe begins on the other side? I'd think about how it all began, how it was created. God created it, of course. But, who created God? God has no beginning and God has no end. How can that be, though? From there, and I don't know how I made this jump, I'd see myself in a casket and wonder, this is horrible, I don't want to be here like this forever. Then, the terrible realization that Oh, God it doesn't matter, I'll be dead. And what is that? Where will that be? Nowhere. Oblivion.

Those thoughts typified nightmarish nights where my heart would beat rapid-fire, sweat pouring down my face and when, terrified, I'd rip the sheets away and run, run, run, out of my bedroom, through the front door and down the street to nowhere.

Now that you've been to other side...

There is no fear.

There was no death in my mother's apartment, no dust, no animals, and no allergies. My mother's house was always clean and dust-free. It was there that Henrietta waited for me to return after every weekend trip to my father's. As I got older, once visitation was determined by my own initiative rather than a court order, I visited my father less and less. Still, although I grew older, I still faced ultimatums.

My father was not allowed to attend my high school or college graduations because he never paid dime one for me and if he came my mother wouldn't. Similarly, he was denied an invitation to my first wedding - yes, my first - because, since he never paid dime one for me and since my mother helped pay for the wedding, the ultimatum was made, if he comes then I won't so make your choice. I always chose my mother. Even as a young man.

Cassandra told me a story once about how my father failed to be at his own mother's bedside when she died. Even as she called out his name, he wouldn't go to her. He was too afraid. Thus, it turned out, there were two women he failed. Was it karma that kept me away from him as he grew older and more helpless, as he cried out desperately for me to no avail? I was too great a coward to be there for him, too afraid to confront his mortality and equally afraid to come to terms with my own. I couldn't and wouldn't see him grow old, suffer or be human. I avoided him, used my mother and Horace as my escape.

On those rare occasions when I did manage to muster up the courage to see him it was only after Cassandra called and implored me to come. It broke my heart to see him, to see my hero unable to walk without help or even to feed himself. It destroyed me inside to see the desperation in his eyes, the fear, the longing.

Each time I said goodbye, I was sure it would be for the last time. Surely, he won't live another month, I would think. I made sure, then, that he knew that I loved him. By 87, the Alzheimer's had hit him full force and I was never quite sure where his mind was: was he performing Ravel's Bolero on stage in 1931? Dancing in the Rainbow Room in the 40's? Did he know who I was? Did he know who he was?

Before I would leave, I'd grab a tuft of his thick gray and black hair and tug it just a bit, just enough for that lost and glazed look in his eyes to briefly disappear, just enough that he would see me through the mist that clogged and handicapped his consciousness, so that he would look in my eyes. At that point when I knew he saw me, even for an instant, when I felt in my soul that he knew who I was, that his son was there, I'd say, "Daddy, I love you. I love you, daddy."

He would smile for a moment and nod before drifting off to whatever ethereal dimension he was dancing in. I knew my father, he was dancing. He would not be wheelchair bound when his spirit could dance somewhere else. My father was performing somewhere, dancing the Flamenco.

His First Visit

When he did finally die, I was sleeping in a tent in North Lake Tahoe with a girlfriend. This would be the first time he would come to me after his passing.

It was 4:30 in the morning when I woke up to see my father standing over me in my tent. He was sweating, and I could see that he was scared. Outside the tent, I heard hoof-beats and the wild neigh of a horse.

"Daddy?" I whispered, astonished to see him.

"Pep," he pleaded, "I need you."

The horse cried out, my father looked over his shoulder in a panic and then, I woke up. What was he running from? Why was he so scared? Was my father running from death, the horse of the Grim Reaper chasing him down? I blinked, and my father was gone.

Was it all just a dream? When I opened my eyes, I found that I was in the same position I was in when my father first entered the tent. Like my father, I usually sleep on my back.

I immediately woke my girlfriend up. She complained and cursed me, calling me crazy for taking down the tent at that early hour and for having to rush home to Los Angeles, thus ending on day one what was supposed to be a four-week cross-country tour and, ending also, what was, in hindsight, one of my many unhealthy relationships.

Eight hours later, I was standing at the porch of my studio apartment in the San Fernando Valley. I knew my girlfriend and I were done, not simply because I backed out of that trip but for a mounting multitude of other divisive reasons. After eight hours of driving, however, I was exhausted and ready to drop. I'll cry about it when I wake up, I thought as I opened the door, sure that I would see a red light flashing on my answering machine, a message from Cassandra.

There was nothing. No flashing. No messages at all. Falling backwards upon my bed and closing my eyes to sleep, I felt like an idiot. Since I obviously won't be on my road trip, I'll visit my daddy in the morning, I thought before passing out.

I slept that entire day and well into the night before my phone rang at about 11:30 pm. Drunk from sleep, I got to the phone too late to answer but my answering machine caught Cassandra's voice letting me know that my father had died earlier that morning. I was shattered by the news, by my father's ghostly visit, but mostly gripped by guilt, a guilt I wouldn't fully shake until I entered that zapateria on the Boulevard of the Dead.

Always with Me

Even before I ran through that fateful red, before I died, my father haunted me. I felt his presence with me always. He was always in my dreams, always making his presence playfully known to me, always trying to get my attention.

Not long after he passed, in fact, he came to me in a lucid dream. Within this dream, I woke in the night to the sounds of clanking pots and pans in my bachelor pad. Rising from bed, I walked through the hallway and into my kitchen where I found my father, young again at sixty, at the stove stirring a pot of his famous picadillo.

Nobody made picadillo like my father. It was his signature meal; a Spanish-style stew with ground beef, tomatoes, all sorts of finely cut vegetables, olives, capers, a dash of oregano and some basil, red wine vinegar and a swig more of red wine. Truly, my father was also an artist in the kitchen. Even today, I make picadillo on special occasions so that I might feel, and that my own children might know, my father's spirit, the essence of their grandfather, in the wondrously delicious odor that saturates our home on these special nights. He looked at me playfully as he stirred the stew and I began to cry.

"I'm sorry, Daddy," I whimpered, "I'm sorry I wasn't there."

He dropped the ladle into the pot, turned and reached out to me. At first, I thought he wanted me to take his hand, but then I saw that what he really wanted was for me to pull his finger.

"No, Daddy," I insisted, "No!"

This was my father the prankster who wanted me to pull his finger so that he could fart. As classy and sophisticated as he was, he delighted in such dirty humor.

"Pull my finger!" he demanded.

"No!"

"Maldita sea!" he growled, "pull my finger and pull it now!"

Reluctantly, I did as my father told me. I pulled his finger and he let out a loud and rapturous fart. Then, he laughed that deep laugh of his, the kind of laugh that invited and seduced anyone who heard it to laugh as well, even if they didn't know what the joke was.

That's how I first knew that my father was okay and that he forgave me. Joking was his way. When I woke up, it was to the faint smell of picadillo in my dark bedroom.

My father haunted me in other ways, as well.

There is a framed picture I have of my father when he was just a boy, posing with a puppy in 1912. I can't count the times that this photo has fallen from its shelf, or the many occasions it would disappear from its spot on the shelf to be discovered somewhere else in the house. These kinds of things occurred often for a while. Just my father, I supposed, trying to get my attention, his fun-loving way of messing with me and saying, Hello.

In the Monterey Bay, before I crashed my Civic, living with my wife in our one-bedroom apartment, my father came to me in a pronounced manner. I was at the kitchen table, writing a screenplay on, interestingly enough, my father's extraordinary life. From the table, I could see into the living room where my wife was laying on the couch, watching a tela-novella. At my feet, Wiggles, our super-hyper miniature Doberman, was uncharacteristically still, looking weirdly paralyzed, staring past me at the blank white wall.

As an aspiring screenwriter, I always made sure I had a white wall nearby, a space with no pictures, just blank, like a movie screen, where I could project and imagine the action of my movie playing out. Wiggles stared at that white wall, mesmerized.

Then, in a burst, Wiggles raced breakneck around my chair several times, so fast that she became a whirring blur about my feet. Abruptly, she would stop, look at the wall then whirl around the chair again.

"What's up with Wiggles?" I asked my wife.

"Dog's crazy," she responded.

Wiggles suddenly stopped on a dime, at the same spot she started from, at my feet, still looking past me at the white wall. Then, she slowly lowered her head so that she now looked directly into my eyes.

As our eyes met, a cold chill descended upon me, as if an icy sheet had fallen softly over my head and shoulders, then through me.

Frightened by the eerie coldness that penetrated me, I leapt from my seat, away from the table, out of the cold. My wife didn't even notice, as she was so immersed in her show. Wiggles slowly turned her head toward me again and I felt that icy chill once more. This time, kitchen lights suddenly flickering, the cold pierced my skin so profoundly that, for whatever reason, I began to cry.

"Daddy," I instinctively cried out, "You're scaring me. Please stop."

With that, it did stop. The lights returned to normal and the cold went away. Wiggles sprang into the living room, curling up on her pillow by the couch. Oblivious to all, my wife fidgeted with the remote, wondering why the television suddenly went off.

I can't say how I knew it was my father's spirit that came to me that night. I just knew it was him. Unlike the dream I had a few years prior, in which he had me pull his finger to trigger a fart, this visit was quite unsettling. While there was no evidence other than a strong sixth sense to prove it, this visit was a foreboding of some kind, a warning; of a marriage crumbling, babies born to a home already broken, or the accident that would take me to the Boulevard of the Dead. Whatever the purpose of this haunting, I was definitely left troubled.

As I leaned over the table to turn off my word processor, I read over the last lines I had written from my script. Was it any coincidence that they came from a scene depicting that early morning visitation in North Lake Tahoe, when my father came desperately into my tent, when I looked up and said, "Daddy?" Indeed, my father's presence was always about me. For now, at least and for whatever reason, he just wouldn't leave me alone.

The Plaster Castle

Seven years after my father died, on the day before the Northridge earthquake in 1994, I met Cassandra for a little hike along the Bridle Path area of Simi Valley, California. We talked a lot on that sunny day, catching up on our lives and sharing memories of my father.

★ ★

I was thirty-four, still struggling financially and scraping by as a teacher and varsity basketball coach. Like my father, I wasn't good with money. I was not a spendthrift, a wastrel or loose with cash. I understood the value of money and I had a certain knack for saving. I just never made enough of it. Money was important but it wasn't everything to me. I certainly wanted more of it but I just couldn't motivate myself to work for money's sake.

I must confess to a darker feeling I had, also, that I didn't deserve money. Like my father, I felt unworthy; not only of attracting a healthy and loving relationship but of having money or abundance in my life.

As a teacher, I never moved up the salary scale. In education, at least in California, where tenure still exists, salaries go up relative to how many college units one takes after a bachelor's degree. The more classes one takes combined with the number of years one teaches, the higher the pay. Salary is not a reflection necessarily of how good a teacher one might be but how long one has been a student. After receiving my credential in 1991, I pledged that I would never sit in on another canned and dry education course again. I would commit myself, rather, to my classroom, my coaching, my writing and my art.

I avoided promotion and I saw a tie as something to be wary of. I never quite trusted the suits. Actually, I've lost count of the many times I was asked to enter administration and invited into the good old boys' club. I'd always say no or back out somehow. I was happy in the comfort zone of the classroom and proud to consider myself one of the last of the real teachers, the crusaders; one who didn't buy in, drink the Kool-Aid, or get watered down and made generic by ever changing buzz words or what was fast becoming a sterilized institution.

Great teachers like Socrates and Jesus would never make it in modern education where teachers are not expected to teach but only facilitate.

I saw No Child Left Behind, as I see Common Core today, as a syndicated conspiracy to destroy Jefferson's dream of a free and public education for all, an evil effort to sabotage public education, dumb it down, and drive everyone to private schools and charters.

All part of the Man in Black's nefarious plans.

Today, as public education in America crumbles and privates thrive, as opportunity and the middle-class deteriorates as a result, it seems that I wasn't far off with my thinking.

★ ★

Hiking with Cassandra on that hot January day in 1994, my situation had not improved. I was stuck and looked to be stuck for a long time. No stability, no direction.

"You're very much like your father," Cassandra began, as we stepped gingerly across a dried creek bed.

We paused along a dusty brown bank and Cassandra reached into her backpack.

"Do you remember that your father built a plaster castle?" she asked.

"Yes," I answered, "when I was little, he promised that he would build me one. He never finished it."

It was an exceptionally warm and dry day, earthquake weather, exactly the type of day people might speak about before a magnitude 6.5 quake. Cassandra felt around and fumbled about within her backpack. I thought she was reaching for a canteen but she pulled out something else.

"Remember this?" she asked, opening her hand to reveal a miniaturized medieval tower made of plaster. It was this same tower I would later see on the altar upon entering the zapateria on the Boulevard of the Dead.

★ ★

"Someday," my father promised me as a child, "I am going to build you a great plaster castle. It will be spread across the entire floor. It will have four towers, walls and a moat. It will be just for you. It will have a little wooden drawbridge, barred windows and doors with handles that open and close."

115

I thought the plaster castle was my father's pipe dream and Big Fish tale. I never dreamed that it ever went further than that.

★ ★

"He finished the castle, Pep," Cassandra said, "it was magnificent. Everything worked; windows and doors opened, the drawbridge went up and down, every brick or stone carved in. There was even water in the moat and a forest surrounding theentire castle."

Amazed, I took the white plaster tower in my hands.

"This is all that's left of it," she continued, "The castle took up almost all the floor space in the garage. It was sprawling. It was perfect. At the end of a long day, though, after working on his castanets, your father decided to close shop. Leaving, he slammed the garage door on his way out. Well, he must have slammed it hard because he heard something fall inside. When he opened the door and flicked on the lights to see what it was that fell, he saw that the entire castle had deteriorated and turned mostly to dust. Everything collapsed, except for this tower."

Cassandra got to her feet, dusted off her butt, and threw the backpack over her shoulder. It was time to head back.

"Weird day," she said, observing the shredded clouds above us, "pretty day, but weird. Like something's about to happen."

It did. The great and tragic Northridge quake of 1994.

★ ★

I almost felt responsible for that quake, as if I had a hand in causing it. Two nights before, on a Friday game night, I coached my High School basketball team to an important win, one that pulled us closer to clinching the first league championship in the 34-year history of the school. During the game, Michael, my brilliant star point guard, fractured his ankle in the closing minutes of play. It was an injury that would take at least six weeks to recover from. With the second half of our season and play-offs on the horizon, knowing that we had no chance whatsoever of winning without Michael, I prayed, Please God, do something.

The Northridge earthquake came three days later, on Martin Luther King Day, the day after my hike with Cassandra. As a result, the season was postponed nearly two months, with our gymnasium being used as a Red Cross center. While it was a horribly catastrophic event, it nevertheless gave us just enough time to get Michael healthy again. By the time our season was resumed, Michael led us to our historic championship and to the L.A. City Play-Offs.

★ ★

Holding the plaster tower, I followed Cassandra down the trail.

"Your father was brilliant, Pep," she said, "but that castle collapsing was so typical of him. He put so much time into this castle. He made sure of each detail, from door handles, to the flags at the top of each tower. In the end, the whole thing just collapsed because he shut the door a bit too hard. Do you know why it fell?"

"Why?"

"After all his demanding work, your father used the wrong kind of base with the plaster. Even though he paid all that attention to details, he used the wrong foundation. That was your father. It was so typical of him. He was one of the greatest Flamenco dancers of all time, he spoke seven languages, choreographed ballets, hobnobbed with the Hollywood elite, wrote poetry, fenced, played polo, carved wood, sang and kept people spellbound with his stories. He was an intellectual, a great lover, a true romantic, a renowned artist."

"I know."

"But he didn't always know."

"He didn't?"

"He was never satisfied, never at peace. In many ways, he just didn't believe in himself. He was married four times and each of his wives left him. No matter how much they loved him it was never enough. They could never prove their love to him. He never believed that they loved him. He just never believed that he was good enough or worthy of being loved. It was a burden he carried with him over the course of several lifetimes."

Cassandra stopped a moment to catch her breath.

"Just like that plaster castle," she continued, "he was such an amazing, beautiful man, but he crumbled in the end for lack of proper foundation. That foundation comes from loving oneself. That's the crazy tragedy of it all. As many gifts as he was blessed with, your father just couldn't truly feel that he was lovable, not by women and not even by God."

My father and I were tormented by the same demons and Cassandra could see it. How else to explain the rocky course of my own life, the dark and frequent bouts with depression, the self-destructive cycles, the unhealthy relationships, the seemingly groundless self-loathing, the yearning to be loved and nurtured and the constant and relentless quest to prove myself worthy.

Like my father and the plaster castle, my life was without a proper foundation. I was incapable of loving myself simply because. I judged myself by my past, by my failures, by my guilt, by my salary, my awards and by the criteria of success established by the illusion itself. I was incapable of loving myself and others unconditionally and simply because. I could not feel worthy. I was the plaster castle that my father built.

You were his son.

It would not be the next day's earthquake, however, that would bring me crumbling down, forcing me to rebuild. No, that would come a year later via a car accident and the ethereal drive that would follow.

Monterey Bay

Now, at 35, my life was still teetering precariously upon a fragile foundation. After surviving the Northridge Quake and winning a championship, I bailed L.A. with my young and future ex-wife for the Monterey Bay.

I was now living in my dream world. While I wouldn't admit it to anyone, however, I was growing bored within the sterile institutional framework of education and already unhappily married after just a few short months.

You would discover that spark for teaching again after your return from the Boulevard of the Dead — now that you knew your purpose, which was to paint the world blue.

By now, I had decided that I was not destined to live out all my dreams, my art would never sell, and that my stories would not be told outside of a classroom or a basketball court.

I told myself, my dreams were wrong, it wasn't meant to be. I was beginning to surrender and buy into the Man in Black's illusion. I just couldn't fight or dream anymore.

I conceded that if indeed I was always to be poor, if I was just going to be a normal guy all my life, if I was never going to experience adventure or travel, if the window for anything extraordinary in my life ever happening had closed, if I was going to be a teacher all my life, if I was going to be mediocre and miserable then, damn it, I would be mediocre and miserable in a place I loved, and I loved the Monterey Bay.

Mediocrity and misery are, as you know, states of mind. As is happiness.

Since the days when my mother and Horace took us all on weekend trips and long drives, I loved it there. My sister and I groaned, of course, when we were thrown into the back seat of the Nova, or later the Colony Park station wagon, dragged away from our friends and my television, for the family drive. Secretly, though, I enjoyed these long excursions to Carmel, Big Sur, Monterey and Santa Cruz. I adored the scenery of the pines, the rich history, the culture, the awesome views from Highway 1, Cannery Row before it became a theme park, the endless blue sea, the otters in the slough, the strolls down Fisherman's Wharf, the smell of caramel corn and smoked salmon, the sea lions barking beneath the pier. I loved especially the Reinstedt books, a classic series of books depicting ghostly tales about the region, which could be purchased at gift shops along the historic Fisherman's Wharf or at nearly any tourist spot in Monterrey.

I left a coaching and teaching job in LA to become the director of an alternative School in Loma with a curriculum designed to modify the behaviors of At-Risk middle school youth. The school was run out of an old Head Start building in Loma, in what was then an overgrown lot once known to the locals as *Pine Park*.

When I accepted a job over the phone with the North Monterey County Unified School District, Loma was not what I had pictured. I had it in my head somehow that North Monterey County was the northern part of the beautiful city of Monterey. I didn't realize it was a separate county north of Monterey. While I won't go into the weir set of circumstances and synchronicities that came together to bring me there, I have no words to convey how deeply my heart sank that first day I reported for work and found myself in the middle of nowhere. Considering how badly I now wanted to surrender and escape back to LA, it is a wonderful irony that I became so deeply enamored with this community.

I had never run a school before, never wanted to. If it wasn't for Mac, my mentor of many years in Los Angeles, I would never have been able to write out the curriculum or design its program. It was Mac, a brilliant and mysterious man in his own right, who developed the curriculum for me based on his own extensive research into the workings of other successful alternative schools. While the curriculum was standards based, the magical world within that school was of my own creation. I called this school, *Valhalla*. It was a unique experiment, seeped in the teachings of Traditional Indian Medicine and my love for Marvel Comics and Thor. While the school site has long since been razed and turned into a beautiful ballpark, *Valhalla* was highly successful, even legendary, at least in the eyes of parents and community who gauged my success by the lives being saved and not by test scores.

While I enjoyed a certain success and fulfillment as director of *Valhalla*, I was horribly unhappy at home. When I met her, my wife was a hot, way too young for me, spirited and saucy Latina. Having lived my own life as a doormat, never able to draw the line or say no to anyone, I found her street smarts and ghetto savvy very attractive. She had attitude to spare and never let anyone take advantage of her or, as she would put it, step all over her as they did to me.

It was ironic, then, that the very attitude I found so attractive at first was the one characteristic that would eventually frustrate me the most.

I knew the minute we arrived in Monterey, sadly even before, that we were a mistake, the greatest mistake of my life.

No mistakes, Pep. You know that now. You chose her.

There was someone else before her. It should have been her.

Your soul mate. You left her behind.

I didn't want to. I just made too many traps for myself. I let her go. I blew it.

No, you didn't. You never let her go, not in your heart, and leaving her behind would not be the end. She was your 'forever' girl. Eventually, she would call out to you through the Quetzal and you would be compelled to find her again.

But that…

Is another story.

For another book.

Through your wife would come your Wise One and your Silent Warrior.

True.

I didn't want to get married. I'd already tried it once with someone closer to my own age and failed miserably. It's just that I wanted to be in Monterey and I didn't have the heart to break up and leave her behind. Being a good Catholic girl, she wouldn't move unless we were married. What else could a highly screwed up and emotionally fractured guy with a noble heart do? Within a week of accepting the job, I asked her parents for her hand then whisked her out to Lancaster for a quick hitch. The next day we were searching for an apartment in a beach town community stuck in the 60's a half hour north of Loma.

I'll go no further into the supreme insecurity that must have motivated me to marry and begin a life with a younger woman so horribly wrong for me. I think I've pretty well covered how messed up I was. With respect for my ex-wife, though, it's best merely to say that we were both terribly mismatched. If we had never had children, I'm sure that we would have broken up, gone our separate ways and would have been happy never to think of each other again. I believe that we were on the very verge of breaking up, close to admitting our mutual unhappiness, when we discovered that she was pregnant. Our relationship was one of perpetual squabble, nit picking, button pushing, lives led on two different intellectual and perceptual levels. I, with my head in the clouds, she with her feet firmly and practically rooted, immovable, to the ground. We were doomed from the start.

October 1ˢᵗ

My wife and I woke up especially early that morning, October 1ˢᵗ at 5 am. We were anxious to pick up a U-Haul truck for the big move back to Santa Cruz. When we first arrived in the Monterey Bay area, we decided on living in Santa Cruz rather than in the town where I worked. However, after one year of living between the beach and the redwoods, my secretary at *Valhalla* offered my wife and I a great deal.

It seemed that my secretary was moving out of her beautiful ranch house in the Loma countryside, less than two miles away from *Valhalla*. Her daughter was going to attend a UC in southern California and she was going to move south with her. The house would be ours to rent if we wanted it and we jumped at the chance.

After three months, though, my secretary was still living in the home while we were relegated to one bedroom. Living quarters became cramped and so by September, it was time to move out and I was set on moving back to Santa Cruz.

Having secured a quaint studio in a beach village south of Santa Cruz, we reserved a U-Haul for the next morning. That's how it came to pass that we were on the road so early, with hardly any rest that night to sharpen my already frazzled state of mind and why I zoned out as we approached that intersection. It is also how I, ultimately, now found myself standing face to face with my father within a tiny zapateria on the Boulevard of the Dead.

★ ★

"Daddy," I spoke to the shadow, "I do know you."

My father emerged from the shadows. He was as I remembered him in happier days. With a smile, he turned and opened a door that led into a darkened room. Passing into the darkness, he motioned with his hand for me to follow.

Inside, my father flicked on the lights and I was treated to a most glorious sight. Spreading out over every inch of a polished hardwood floor was a magnificent white plaster castle; a sparkling watery moat surrounding high walls, a drawbridge at the center of each wall, flags at the tops of four towers.

The door suddenly slammed shut behind us, so hard that the earth shook beneath the floorboards. The room rocked for a moment and I braced myself against the wall. Amazingly, as the earth finally settled, I saw that the plaster castle was still perfectly intact; not a crack on it nor a wall or tower turned to dust.

"I've been working hard," my father proudly whispered, motioning to the wooden jaguar I still held in my hand, "Your Tia's sopa was delicious."

In that supernatural moment when my father showed me the magnificent plaster castle he had constructed in Heaven, I knew, after many lifetimes of suffering, that he was finally healed. That he had let go of the guilt and negativity that, although he knew so much professional success, kept him from finding true fulfillment in his life.

Standing over the plaster castle he fashioned in the afterlife, my father saluted me, the salute of the Ghost Warrior; tapping his forehead with his fist - I saw the mole.

My father had a mole on his left hand, to the left of his thumb and between the wrist and the index finger. It is the same mole I have on my own hand. The same mole my daughter bares on hers. The same mole I saw for some reason on the old painter's hand as well.

From his forehead he pounded his fist hard upon his chest and then lifted his open hand to the heavens.

★ ★

Again...

The Salute of the Ghost Warrior
The fist to the forehead indicated the fight for the Mind...
We are warriors of Mind, because we
fight to learn...

The fist pounding hard upon the chest symbolized the fight for the Body...

We are warriors of Body because we fight
to keep our Bodies strong...

And the open hand to the universe a symbol for the fight for Spirit...

We are warriors of spirit because we fight
To keep alive the Seven Sacred Aspects of;
Respect, Humility, Compassion, Truth,
Honesty, Unconditional Love and Wisdom

I have taught this salute and the Seven Sacred Aspects to all my students and basketball players over the years. Once upon a time, before each practice or class, it had been ritual for both players and students to salute as Ghost Warriors and to recite the following creed;

We are Warriors of Mind, Body and Spirit. We are Warriors of Mind because we fight to Learn. We are Warriors of Body because we fight to keep our bodies strong. We are Warriors of Spirit because we fight to keep alive the Seven Sacred Aspects of Respect, Humility, Compassion, Truth, Honesty, Unconditional Love and Wisdom.

* **Respect** *comes with the realization that the light shining in our eyes is the same light that shines in the eyes of all men.*
* **Humility** *means that we all shine with the same intensity and no one man shines brighter than the next.*
* **Compassion** *means that we are sensitive to the suffering of others.*
* **Honesty** *means that we are truthful.*
* **Truth** *is that which we innately know to be true.*
* **Unconditional Love** *means that we love ourselves and others simply because we are all of the same light.*
* **Wisdom** *is the knowledge we gain from the mistakes that we make along the road to discovering the light that burns within us.*

★★

Paint the World Blue with Your Stories

Before my time on the Boulevard of the Dead was done, my father whispered one more message. It was another affirmation about my dreams, my purpose, my destiny and my divine plan.

"Paint the world blue, Pep," he said, "paint the world blue with your stories. Fight the Man in Black!"

There are many ways to heal people. While I never cured cancer with a touch, brought sight to a blind man, nor led the lame to walk, I hope that as a teacher, coach or artist, my storytelling might have healed kids, mended hearts, and inspired some to strive for their highest potential. I believe that is my calling.

I would soon be leaving the Boulevard of the Dead and upon my return to the Land of the Living I would embark on a new quest, a clearly defined and divinely directed mission to paint the world blue, to be the Ghost Warrior and to expose the illusion of a certain Man in Black.

"I love you," my father whispered, staring deep and lovingly into my eyes.

"I love you," I told him.

With one last salute my father disappeared. This was the goodbye my father and I never shared. This time it was right. While I still cried, it wasn't out of mourning but rather of gratitude for a second chance, for the opportunity to reconnect with my hero, to seal the bond between father and son forever. They were cathartic tears celebrating the deep and instinctive knowledge that my father never died, that no one ever really dies, that his spirit was still very much and literally alive outside of the illusion that had kept us apart.

Your father lives still in the Quetzal.

My Guardian Angel

Wiping away tears, I turned to see my own reflection in a mirror on the far wall. While it was surely me, reflected in the glass, the image in the mirror had a life of its own. There were no tears on this face, but instead a reassuring smile and on my head I wore my signature brown cap, the same one that the old painter wore. To my surprise, my own likeness hailed me over, gesturing with his hand to come nearer.

Drawn to my own reflection, I stepped gingerly across the floor, careful not to knock over any part of the castle. As I neared my own reflection in the glass, my likeness saluted me Ghost Warrior style.

Then, a wondrous metamorphosis occurred over my image as I saw my face morph, first, into that of my nine-year-old self, the boy in the striped shirt and the tuft of black hair on his bald head, traumatized by the divorce of his parents, the boy who hid out from the world in his own head, drawing and watching television in a darkened bedroom.

"I love you," the boy said with a smile. I felt that warm electrical rush course through me.

Quickly, the boy's features began to wither and age, the hair growing long and gray to the shoulders. This was the face of the ghost I hid from since I was a child, the High Priest of Palenque in my dreams, the old painter who looked so familiar to me but whose face I just couldn't place, the old man who guided me along the Boulevard of the Dead, directed me to each shop along the way and facilitated the meetings between me and the ghosts of my past. It was the old painter's face I saw now in the mirror. Here was the man whose voice I tuned out since childhood but finally heard amid the din of petty human drama on the Pagaro Bridge. He was the me I would become. Here was my guardian angel.

The clues were there all along and yet I didn't see them; my brown cap, the mole on the old painter's hand, the deep and hearty laugh, the painter's overalls, the brushes and the blue paint. Yes, the clues were there from the beginning that this old painter, this guardian angel, was me.

Indeed. It was always you.

*My Soul Retrieved
A Ghost Warrior Born*

As it turned out, I was my own guardian angel. It was my own timeless and eternal spirit that came to me as a child, the voice of the Mayan High Priest and warrior I once was and will always be, that spoke to me in my dreams and whispered to me in the darkness, my own spirit reaching out to me, fighting through an illusion cast upon humanity by the Man in Black and his Architects of Deception, leading me into the peace and oneness of the Quetzal. It was that most enduring aspect of me coming to me, my highest self, trying to reconnect me with the divine light-sonic vibration of my own truth, with my divine origins and my creator.

It was all GOD.

The jade jaguar, my nagual, my power animal and spirit guide were yet another angel and aspect of myself. As a boy, I was afraid of this jaguar that prowled about my bedroom at night and whose shadow loomed like a boogeyman ready to pounce upon me from my wall. I didn't know then that the jaguar came from within me, a primordial extension of my own spirit, there by my side to protect me and guide me in this world and in the spirit world.

It wasn't the jaguar that followed us through the Boulevard of the Dead but we who followed it.

With this magical revelation, I felt the greatest blast of warmth yet. Somehow, I finally felt whole again …for the first time. Certainly, it was the most complete, whatever complete means, I had ever felt. Revitalized by this electric charge, I now saw the face in the mirror begin to dissolve and as it did I could gradually see my own thirty five-year-old visage begin to reemerge. Somewhere in the room, I heard the jade jaguar growl.

"Paint the world blue, Pep," the old painter said, his face disappearing altogether so that I now stared at my own more recognizable reflection.

"Paint the world blue, Pep," I heard the old painter say from somewhere in the darkened room, "and lead the revolution. Be the Ghost Warrior!"

"Paint the world blue," I repeated to myself in the mirror before closing my eyes.

For a moment, there was only blackness and in that darkness I must have departed the Boulevard of the Dead for the very next thing I remember was opening my eyes to the face of that young nurse in the hospital, materializing from a strange blue haze. I had returned to the Land of the Living.

THE LAND OF THE LIVING

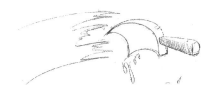

Paint the world blue, the last words I spoke before I left the Boulevard of the Dead and the first words I uttered, according to a young nurse, when I opened my eyes in the Land of the Living. She was the same young nurse who wouldn't tell me, upon regaining consciousness in the hospital, if I were to live or die.

It would take nearly a year to fully recover from the accident. I spent two weeks in the hospital, shot up with so much morphine and Demerol that, for the first 3 days of consciousness, I didn't even feel that my body was broken. I was convinced I'd be back on the basketball courts within a couple days.

The Pretty Nurse

Before I was released to recuperate at home, that pretty nurse, whose name I never caught, came in one day. This nurse had dark Indian features and a bhindi on her forehead by the third eye.

"You're a teacher," she said, as she helped me from my bed so that I could begin a painful but necessary regimen of walking.

"Yeah," I answered, my chest heaving and wheezing, a chest tube sticking out from my ribs, "I'm the director of an Opportunity school in Loma."

She meant something else.

"Not what you do. What you are," she continued.

I was breathing so hard, my chest cavity so full of fluid, I had to pause even before taking my first step.

"I came by your room earlier," she explained, "you were talking in your sleep. You kept repeating the same thing over and over. You kept saying, paint the world blue."

I still didn't fully understand the significance of the message. All my life I'd heard the message but never understood its meaning. Until now. This pretty nurse was about to let me know.

"Blue is a color of enlightenment," she went on, "so, painting the world blue means to teach people, to enlighten people, to open their hearts to truth."

All my life I had wondered about the meaning of my father's words. Even on the Boulevard of the Dead, nobody explained it. What did my father mean when he directed me to paint the world blue? I didn't know. For me, that was always a mystery. Now, two weeks after my return to the Land of the Living, it was this pretty nurse who revealed this meaning to me.

"You are a teacher and a healer," she told me, "It is time for you to get to work."

An Angel, too?

A couple months after I left the hospital, my wife and I visited the third floor looking for that pretty nurse. I brought flowers and wanted to thank her for inspiring me, for helping me to heal, and for solving a mystery that had haunted me since I was a child. Strangely, we couldn't find her and, while we described her to the administration, no one matching her description worked at that hospital. Was she an angel too? I have seen enough now in my life to know that all things are truly possible. At any rate, whoever or whatever she may have been, she came as an angel to me.

A Painful Rehab

The remainder of my rehabilitation would be as an outpatient. Taking my place on the couch in our new apartment, I was far from healed. Still in a neck brace, a broken clavicle, busted ribs, fluids in my chest cavity, my body was a complete wreck and I was in constant pain. I had lost near forty pounds since the day of the accident and I shuffled at a snail's pace about the small apartment. It was allergy season and my broken ribs writhed in agony every time I sneezed or coughed, a pain no amount of Vicodin could take the edge off.

Worst of all, fluids continued to build in my chest cavity, compressing my punctured lung and making it difficult to breathe. At night, the pressure on my lungs was so great that I had no choice but to sleep upright. At one point, the fluid build-up worsened to such an insufferable degree that I returned to the hospital to have nearly two liters of this toxic dark pus painfully siphoned out from my back.

My wife stuck with me throughout my recuperation and bore our first child during it all. While she made it her mission to destroy me after our divorce, there is no doubt that she kept me alive back then. Like I said, my rehabilitation was a long and painful ordeal. She was there to take care of me, even while she was entering the third trimester of her pregnancy.

Emotions ran crazy the first part of that new year and I found myself crying a lot. There were, admittedly, times when I questioned why I was alive. Times when it was difficult to reconcile with what seemed the random nature of my survival.

Down deep, you knew there was nothing random about your survival.

I should have known better. Still, I found myself crying a lot. I cried for everything it seemed. I would cry over the green on a leaf, the whistle of our tea kettle, for the joy of being able to breathe.

Although my angel had assured me over and over that I had a long life left to live, while I was blessed with concrete affirmations of my mission to paint the world blue, there were many moments, I am embarrassed to admit, where I was just plain afraid.

"Wow," people would say upon my recovery, "you did a great job. Congratulations. You pulled through. You were very brave."

I always laugh. What great job did I do? Congratulations for what? What bravery did I exhibit? In fact, I exhibited the exact opposite of bravery when confronted with the possibility of death. I whined and cried every day. At thirty-five years old, I called my mommy every day just to hear her say, "No, Pep, you're not going to die. You're going to be fine."

I told you the same.

What choice did I have but to survive? I certainly didn't want to die... again. Not yet.

You were much more concerned with the pain you were enduring than you were of dying.

For many years later, I would experience, some confusing, reality challenged moments – times when I wasn't sure whether I was alive or dead. I remember, for instance, a driving incident just outside Loma. I was plodding along as I have a habit of doing in the slow lane, admiring the view of the Monterey Bay, divinely surreal with shafts of white light streaking through hovering clouds to touch the placid surface of the water below, when another car cut recklessly in front of me, nearly knocking me off the road. Somehow swerving onto the shoulder of the road, my back tires catching a little gravel, I managed with steady hands and quick reaction to avert what would have been another major accident.

"Whew!" I thought, my heart pumping only after the fact and butterflies swarming my belly, "that was close." In the distance, I could see the speeding car wildly crossing lanes near the top of the grade.

Cue the flashbacks of an earlier accident, when I thought I had avoided disaster but found myself instead in another dimension on the way to Heaven.

"Wait," I asked myself out loud, glancing at the passenger seat, looking for an older version of myself in overalls and for paint buckets, "Am I alive or dead?"

Still Always with Me

The phone rang a few times before I answered it.

Back on my couch, recovering from the accident in our new apartment, I was having one of those bad days, convinced that the fluids would never drain from my chest, that pneumonia was setting into my lungs, that I would never heal and that I would soon be back on my way down the Boulevard of the Dead.

Propped upright in front of the television, my shirt drenched from sweat after breaking yet another fever, groggy from Vicodin, I finally picked up the telephone.

"Hi, Pep," it was my sister's voice.

"Hi," I answered, on the verge of tears again for whatever reason. Like I said, I couldn't always explain my tears. Certainly, I was surprised to hear this cheerful voice. I hadn't heard from my sister in more than a year.

★ ★

My Sister

There are two old home movies from the early sixties that show my sister and I playing together, and with friends, at two different birthday parties when we were very little, no more than four and five. We were two beautiful little angels completely oblivious of our parent's disintegrating marriage or of the divorce that was soon to crush us, scar us and set the tense and fragile tone of our relationship forever. The films show my mother, young and beautiful, hosting birthday parties at our modest home in Silver Lake, California and at the nursery school we attended. My father, a pipe in his mouth threw out candies to the kids and managed the piñata.

Even as small children, the camera reveals how opposite my sister's nature was from my own. At four, my sister was all about the camera. She knew where it was all the time and made sure she was at the center of every shot. If the camera was on me or someone else, she'd find her way into the picture and steal the attention. It wasn't malicious or nasty, it was simply her nature. Even then she had a glow about her, an effervescent presence that commanded attention.

It is no wonder that my sister became a television personality, a highly respected television journalist, one of the ten most influential Latinas in the country, a celebrity. By the time of my accident, she had already received several Emmy awards as a television journalist and anchor.

If anything, I avoided the camera. These old films show me somewhere in the background or off to the corner of the shot, already retreating from the world with my cowboy pistols and rocking horse, pretending to be the Lone Ranger or Roy Rogers, already lost and living in my head.

From childhood, our relationship had always been a rocky one. We handled divorce very differently. We both needed a safe and loving foundation to get us through the chaos. Mostly, we both wanted the attention of our parents. My sister was and is still, loaded with superhuman drive and sparkling personality. She can light up a room just by walking into it. She is bold, daring and outgoing. On the other hand, I was painfully shy and introverted as a child. While I'm still very shy and reclusive in many ways today, I have learned to embrace the spotlight on occasion with my storytelling, coaching and motivational speaking.

I sense, when my sister concluded, rightly or wrongly, that I was the favorite child between my mother and Horace, that she sought out the affection of our father. Remember, I had somewhat abandoned my father in favor of a younger dad and dust-free living. It must have hurt my sister terribly when, after making all the effort toward my father, lavishing him with love and frequent visits, he constantly asked about me.

In the Latino culture, the boy is an important and highly romanticized accomplishment to a man. To be sure, it is the boy who carries on the father's name. I'm sure that this machismo ethic, another aspect of the lie, played a part in my father's favoritism towards me, but there might have been another factor as well. It might simply have been that my father just thought I needed him more. That's what Cassandra believed.

"Pep," Cassandra told me one day, long after his passing, "your father loved both you and your sister equally. But, he felt something about the two of you. He felt that your sister was stronger and that she would be able to handle herself. He told me before he died, he made me promise, he said, 'Take care of Pep,' because he's not as strong as his sister."

I'll admit that I was probably, for whatever reason, a bit more emotionally fragile than my sister, a bit more helpless than her in my youth, certainly more prone to retreating, giving up and falling apart. Maybe that's why he always came to me after his passing. Maybe he still felt, from the spirit world, that I needed him more. In this, we may have found the answer to one of my sister's most frequently asked questions; why does he always come to you? Why do you always have these experiences and I don't?

Just as Cassandra took care of my father, and as she saved and cared for lost animals all her life, she took care of me and my own children after the devastating effects of an all too predictable divorce left me jobless, homeless and penniless. She was there to give me a home and to keep my family together.

"I can't accept this," I remember telling Cassandra on the day she offered me one of the three homes she owned.

"It's yours," she said, "for you and the kids."

"I can't."

"You must," she reiterated, "your father told me to give this to you."

My father had already been gone from this earth for thirteen years by then, but I knew what she meant. I knew then that my father was about her as he had always been about me. I accepted. How could I refuse?

While I escaped the pain, as a child, by shutting the world out and living in my head, the sad little boy locked up in his room, with the shades down, the television on, drawing superheroes, my sister escaped into the world. If she wasn't going to get the attention and love she craved at home, she'd find it outside the home. Find it she did.

My sister has lived an extraordinary life. She has known both glory and scandal, interviewed great people, travelled the world and witnessed history through her profession. I was never jealous of her success, for even when our relationship was at its most turbulent, I always wished her well and for her continued achievement. There were times, though, when I wished I was more like her; gutsier, more outgoing. I can also say that I would have loved to travel as extensively as she had and in so doing have had the chance to see all the things in the world I dreamed of seeing when I was a boy.

Although we loved each other deeply, we just never seemed to get it right. Every five years or so, we'd get together, enter a business venture together, sabotage ourselves, then take another break from each other again. The scars of divorce and division were deep, the patterns so hard to break. I wished with all my heart that things had been different, that we could have been that dynamic brother-sister duo that could share our families and work together. I am still hopeful, at the time of this writing, that there is time to heal these wounds and enjoy the rest of this life as family. After all, one never knows when one might run another red.

★ ★

It really was a surprise then to hear my sister's voice on that dreadful day, propped up painfully on my couch. Up until then, it was just another hopeless day when I thought I was going to die again.

"I want you to wake up early tomorrow," she said over the phone, "I'm going to be interviewing one of the people on your list, live!"

My list. When my sister first received the nod to host and pioneer the a popular weekend morning news show, she asked me for a list of ten people that I would want her to interview. It was a grand list.

Pep's List:

- Sean Connery
- Muhammad Ali
- Charles Bronson
- Clint Eastwood
- Johnny Carson
- Michael Jordan
- Magic Johnson
- Harrison Ford
- Francis Ford Coppola

The tenth person was an author I had seen recently on the *Larry King Show*. In her bestselling book she chronicled her life communicating with the dead.

Nearly one year after giving her my celebrity wish list, my sister was going to interview one of the people I requested. Who, she wouldn't say. She simply directed me to have my television on at 6 am the next morning,

"You will be very surprised," she told me.

The next morning, believe it or not, I overslept, waking up ten minutes after six. Already upright on the couch, I fumbled through my blankets for the remote control, fearing that I had missed the interview.

I tuned in at the exact moment the interview began. There, on live television for the world to see, my sister sat opposite the author who spoke to the dead. I'm sure that, somewhere in some network vault, or on You Tube, a tape of this interview exists, but for now I must recount for you its proceedings as I did my journey down the Boulevard of the Dead - from memory.

The author spoke about her new book and about life as a medium, of her own Native American spirit guide and of speaking to the dead. Her message; people don't die, our loved ones don't leave us, their spirits are always around and that she speaks with them. Then, the interview took an unexpected turn.

"Do you see anyone around me?" my sister asked the author.

"I do," she answered.

"Who?"

"I see a lean man, dressed in black…"

Dressed in black? Was the devil hovering about that sound stage, lingering with menace about my sister? No. the author was speaking of another man in black.

"He is a dancer, I believe. He may be your father."

My sister seemed stunned. This was not scripted.

"He wants you to know that he loves you very much."

My sister needed to hear that. I feel she waited all her life to hear that, given that she always thought I was the favorite and that our father didn't love her. Indeed, she once described herself as being no more than a pickle on his plate. The deep impact of that moment was apparent on the screen. Yes, my sister, your daddy loved you \and does so still from the other side. I could see that my sister was moved, almost to tears, but she carried on bravely.

"He loves you," the author continued, "but right now he is concerned over your brother who was in some sort of accident recently and is scared and confused."

I gasped.

My father had come to me many times since his passing but never like this. Our loved ones reach out to us in so many ways. Sometimes, they come through to us in our dreams, as specters in the hallway, as a knocking on a wall, or by tipping over a picture frame. Maybe, also, they come to us through the flickering flame of a candle or flashing lights, or the static on the T.V. or radio. Maybe they meet us on a fog shrouded boulevard after we die. Of course, if your sister is a popular television journalist, they might speak through a psychic on live television to deliver a healing message. All they want, I imagine, is to be remembered by us – as death only really comes when they are forgotten, when their stories are not told anymore. Maybe, they come to us out of love, to ease our pain, to validate the immortality of our own souls, to help us to let them go. They might even be asking us to assist them in letting us go so that they may cross that last intersection on their own Boulevard of the Dead into the light of Heaven.

"He wants your brother to know," the author went on, "that he's going to be just fine and that he is always with him."

It wasn't all just my imagination, then. My father coming to me in the tent at the moment of his passing, the lucid dream of him making picadillo and farting in my kitchen, the haunting in my Santa Cruz apartment, seeing him in the zapateria on the Boulevard of the Dead for another paint the world blue moment. It was all real and validated for me yet again by this author.

From that morning on, I was on my way to being just fine. That television moment brought it all together for me. Now, I truly believed I was going to get better.

Even that spectacular occurrence would not be my father's last effort to reach out to me. Indeed, he would come to me one last time. Always the showman, my father would top himself with one final curtain call before crossing over permanently to Heaven.

The Silent Warrior

My daughter, the wise one, was born March 5, 1996. She was born a smaller version of the little girl with garlands that I saw in the fog drenched field, a china doll with perfect pristine features. To be sure, it was my father who delivered her to me, like a proud father walking his own daughter down the aisle. She was the most beautiful baby I had ever seen and, for me, it was love at first sight.

At that point in my life, I didn't want another child. I wanted Rosemarie to be the one and only. I didn't want her to go through what my sister and I had suffered. I didn't want Rosemarie to have to ever compete for her parent's love, never wanted her to feel less than number one on her daddy's list. As I was to learn, life holds many surprises and, within a daddy's heart, there's always room for two number ones or even more.

By August, my wife announced that she was pregnant again. At first, I couldn't believe it. We were already struggling financially. How, I thought, would we be able to manage two kids on a teacher's salary?

"Everything happens for a reason," my mother told me, "it'll all be okay, you'll see."

I thus embraced the idea of another child coming into our lives. When we found out the baby would be a boy, I became even more excited. Now, I would have a boy to carry on my father's name. We would have the perfect pair, a boy and a girl. The arrival date was projected for April 15, 1997.

"That's my father's birthday." I told her, "That's awesome. We must make sure we keep that date. We have to make sure my boy is born on my father's birthday."

"Calm down, Pep," she responded, "No one can be 100% sure that the baby will be born on that day."

Maybe she was right, maybe there were no guarantees that my son would positively, be born on my father's birthday but it would not be for lack of effort on my part.

"Visualize," I counseled her, "see the date, and imagine our son being born on April 15. Come on, make it happen!"

I drove my wife crazy with what became an obsession to have my boy born on my father's birthday.

"Give it a rest," she complained, "he'll come when he comes."

Indeed, he came when he came, and he didn't come on April 15th. On that day, my wife still hadn't even had one labor pain. Okay, I comically lectured to myself, I guess I'll have to love him anyway. I would be just as elated when he was born two days later, on April 17th.

Unlike Rosemarie, who came out of the womb fully formed, faultless and beautiful, Dylan arrived like a squiggling plate of pasta come to life. He was the weirdest looking thing I had ever seen. His frail, formless and jaundiced body looked like a heaping pile of noodles, his tiny head was pointed, his ears flattened, and his face dominated by the biggest lips I had ever seen. I would have never guessed by looking at him then that my boy would grow up to be as handsome as he has become today.

"He's here!" I told Cassandra on the phone, calling her from the birthing suite.

I could hear Cassandra crying tears of joy over the phone.

"Sorry he wasn't exactly born on the 15th," I told her, "but the 17th is just as good."

"What's so big about the 15th?" she asked.

"My father's birthday."

"The 15th isn't your father's birthday, Pep, today is! Your father was born on the 17th!"

I don't recall that my father ever celebrated his birthday. Instead, he celebrated his Saint's Day, which was St. Joseph's Day. On that day, he would make us his famous picadillo, drink a glass of wine and tell stories of the golden age of Hollywood, the year he played the Rainbow Room for Nelson Rockefeller, his record breaking rendition of Ravel's Bolero at the Hollywood Bowl and those times when he'd pal around with Orson Welles and other stars.

knew, though, that his birthday was sometime in April and the 15th, I guess because taxes are due on that date, always stuck out in my mind. I never did know the date of my father's birthday. Now, holding my own boy in my arms, overwhelmed by the presence of my father's spirit in the room, he made sure, in his own way, that I would never forget the day he was born.

The God Stick

Just as Rosemarie saw angels, Dylan had his own spiritual inclinations. His spiritual awareness was made dramatically apparent to me one day on a trip to Ojai.

The first three years after divorce were spent raising my children pretty well by myself. With their mother living up her new freedom, the kids were mostly with me. It was just me and them.

It was certainly a most challenging time in my life that, ironically, I never wanted to end. I loved being with my kids, doing the daddy thing, reading to them, teaching them basketball, bathing them, putting them to bed with songs and making them lunches for school. I loved every miserable moment of single fatherhood. I went everywhere with them. It was as if I carried my kids in my back pocket. I even took them on job interviews. Surprisingly, rather than hurt my chances, dragging them along landed me a job.

Most of all, I loved hopping into my car with my kids, and taking off on day trips. Since returning to Southern California as a single divorced father, away from the beaches and redwoods of Santa Cruz, my favorite getaway was now Ojai. In Ojai, I'd often go to a place called Meditation Mount where I'd sit on a bench at the end of a nature trail that overlooked the entire Ojai Valley and meditate.

On one of these meditations, I had Rosemarie and Dylan wait for me safely nearby at separate points on the trail. I instructed them to stay where I placed them, not to wander off and, please, not to fight.

Taking off my shirt and sitting on the bench at the end of the trail, I took in the magnificent view. On this day in October, a fluorescent pink fog blanketed the entire valley. The day was beginning to heat up under a warm sun, the mystical pink mist beginning to burn away. Eventually, I closed my eyes, took four deep breaths and began my meditation.

My kids were perfectly behaved, allowing me my meditation without messing around, fighting or even leaving their assigned spots. After meditating, I made my way back to them, coming upon Dylan first. He waited patiently for me beneath a tree, a stick in his hands.

"This is my God-stick," he told me, proudly brandishing his prize. *My God-stick.*

"Your God-stick?" I asked. It was the very same stick the old painter used to stir blue paint as he directed my path along the Boulevard of the Dead.

Dylan nodded.

"God speaks to me through it."

"He does? What does he say?

"She," he sternly corrected, "says that we shouldn't kill bugs."

Through that stick, Dylan sensed the much-neglected feminine aspect of divine creation, an awareness for the masculine/feminine duality of all things and a respect for life.

No Accident

In Dylan struggling with his health so quietly through that first month of life, I saw a silent warrior. Indeed, while he is a chatty and relentlessly playful fellow today, he carries all his hurt and damage quietly in what his best friend calls, the Dylan Box, that isolated far-off place in his mind he retreats to when the pressures of his young life overwhelm him, that place where he doesn't have to feel, where he can go numb. I guess, in a way, like father like son, he lives much of his life in his head as well. In that box, he wages a silent war against all the pain that divorce has wrought upon him.

It is for Dylan that I wrote this lullaby.

Silent...
My little silent warrior,
Fighting the quiet battle...
Riding into war...
Onto silent battlefields.

Silent...
Silent warrior...
Through your veins flows the blood
Of silent warriors past,
Scars seared into their hearts,
Fighting yourself everyday...
Between choices...
right or wrong.
Fighting...
With all your might
To defend and do...

What is right...
You are older
Than your age...
You're as old as...
The blood...
That flows through your veins...
Older still if...
You trace the light
That shines from your eyes.

Silent...
Silent warrior...
My little silent warrior...

Dylan.

A Frightful Night

A few months after Dylan acquired his God-stick, I found him crying in his bed at night. When I sat down to comfort him I saw that he was terrified. In his tear-soaked eyes I sensed the same horror that I experienced as a young boy when I began to think too deeply, when I first became aware that nobody lives forever.

"I don't want you to die," Dylan sobbed.

As a father, I was momentarily rattled. What parent could stand to see their children so deeply shaken? Whatever it was that got Dylan thinking too much and too deep that night, I'll never know, but it could not have been much different from the thoughts that shook me so profoundly as a child when I looked out my bedroom window into the star splattered night sky.

"I'm not going to die, Dylan," I answered him, holding him tight, but that did nothing to console his fear.

"I don't want to die!" he continued.

"Dylan," I told him, "I'm not going to die until I'm ready. I'm going to be here for awhile. So are you."

"But I don't want to die at all. I don't want us to die."

Before the God stick found its permanent spot on our fireplace, Dylan kept it on his bed stand. I took the God stick in my hands and crawled into the covers with Dylan.

"Did you know that I've been to Heaven?"

"You have?" Dylan was surprised.

"Well, I was pretty close."

"What was it like?"

"What I remember was very beautiful. Someday I'll tell you the whole story."

"Tell me now," he demanded as he reached for his God stick, his anxiety receding.

"When you're older," I continued, "maybe I'll even write a book about it."

"With pictures?"

"Of course. Someday, I want to go back to Heaven and stay."

"Not now though, right?" Dylan, clutching his God stick tightly, looked as if he might cry again.

I held my son tighter now and kissed his forehead.

"Nope," I assured him, "We've got too many things I want to do here. But, someday, when we're ready, we'll all want to go back to Heaven."

"Back to Heaven?" Dylan asked, his tears drying slightly, "You mean we've been there before? I don't remember."

★ ★

Not long ago, one of my closest friends, Paul, recounted to me a tale that relates well here. It seems that shortly after the birth of his nephew, his family hosted a dinner party to celebrate the birth. Among the guests was a young married couple with a two-year-old boy of their own.

After dinner, everyone relaxed around the living room to chat and loosen their belts. At some point, the young couple realized that their son was no longer playing with Legos behind their chair and they began to search for him. As they were unable to locate him immediately, the whole party embarked on a frantic search for the young boy.

Hearing voices from the intercom connected to the newborn's bedroom, the party rushed upstairs to find the boy hanging over the baby's crib and whispering in its ears.

"Tell me what Heaven is like," the boy implored the baby, "I'm beginning to forget."

★ ★

"Yes, Dylan," I explained to my traumatized son, "We all come from Heaven. Most of us forget. We chose the lives that we are living. In Heaven, you chose to be here with me. Eventually, you'll remember again and then you'll go back."

"Don't forget to write the book," he said with a yawn.

Here it is.

Somehow, I was able to quell Dylan's fears that night and it wasn't long before he was fast asleep in my arms. On that night, I thanked God for the journey I took down the Boulevard of the Dead several years before, for the blessing of knowing exactly what to tell my child that night.

No Coincidence

Cassandra was convinced for a time that Dylan must have been the reincarnation of my father. Honestly, I never believed that. I did sense, though, that my father, from the spirit world, assisted by whatever angels, had a playful hand somehow in the orchestration, and timing, of my son's birth. He brought Dylan to me in much the same manner he brought Rosemarie to me; a little girl with garlands in a field. The one thing I do not believe is that any of this was all just coincidence. This was my father, by grace of God, saying goodbye one last time in the big and dramatic manner befitting the way he lived his life and now the way he lives in the afterlife. I knew he was laughing. This was my daddy affirming for me, again, what I had known instinctively since the day that he died. Whether in life or on the Boulevard of the Dead, he had always been there, looking after me. Between he and my guardian angel, who was me, I had never been alone. We are never alone. There is a universe that loves us, a God that reaches out to us through the Quetzal who wants to save us all.

PAINTING THE WORLD BLUE

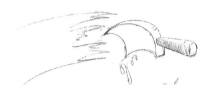

As I sit here today behind my art desk, more than twenty years after the accident that took me to the other side, I find myself embracing the Ghost Warrior I was destined to be, called to be; fighting each day to live out my divine plan and expose the truth about the illusion. I fight to block out the noise that would quash my own voice and cut my connection to the Quetzal. It is a war I wage for the right to my own soul, to pain the world blue.

This account of my near death and my rebirth is itself a part of my own dreamquest, a bold and passionate pursuit to live out my purpose and join others within the consciousness shifting vibration of the Quetzal in a spiritual revolution against a bogus and manufactured reality. In this way, a new awareness and paradigm will eventually be ushered forth; one that liberates all people from the shackles of the wicked Man in Black's lie. It is as a Ghost Warrior, then, an artist with many brushes, that I play out my own divine purpose, and paint the world blue.

Life didn't suddenly become perfect simply because I died, came back and knew better. As M. Scott Peck states so eloquently in his classic, *The Road Less Travelled*, a book that Jake once gave me and everyone else he knew as a Christmas gift, "Life is difficult."

I still battle the illusion…

We all do.

I fight myself from surrendering to the illusion and losing my soul to it and to a material world. I cannot fall into that River of the Damned.

146

The Man in Black's illusion is supported by various instruments of deception...

All of which we will discuss in depth in our next book.

... they are set in motion when we are closest to achieving our dreams, which are part of God's Will. These are the times when we suffer setbacks, when dreadful things seem to happen.

A break up, car troubles, losing a job, money problems...

Anything that disrupts our momentum, where we lose faith, give up and fall back into the illusion; This is where negativity takes over, when cycles of anger, hopelessness, depression, and other petty worldly concerns consume us and conspire to destroy us.

Issues of morality, success, race, religion, self-image, competition are all manufactured by the Man in Black and all designed to control the masses by addicting us all in his illusion. All designed to stop us.

The illusion is strong. We were born into it, our faith in it so hard to shake.

We are at our strongest when we keep relentless focus on our dreams and their purpose.

I am strongest when I maintain a disciplined Ghost Warrior lifestyle; which includes daily meditation and prayer, a plant-based diet and exercise. This works for me. This lifestyle fortifies me with the strength to fight for my dreams. Again, I will discuss this lifestyle in greater depth in my next book.

Our next book.

I find that my own Ghost Warrior way offers me the most effective approach to connecting with the Quetzal...

Allowing for a more fluid discourse between you and I...

...And God, of course.

Of course, living in this manner, we hear our own voices most clearly.

Today, I am still a teacher and a basketball coach, still drawing, telling stories and writing. At the time of this writing, my children, Rosemarie the Wise One and Dylan, the Silent Warrior, have grown into young adults.

If, indeed, Rosemarie was sent here to teach me how to love then it was in the process of letting go and in truly loving unconditionally that the lesson has been most profound. By 13, the Wise One, already ferociously independent, was letting me know that she was not me and that she already had her own path separate from what I may have wanted for her. Today, because of a perfect storm of circumstance and a couple parental blunders, Rosemarie has well rejected "my way." She's out there blazing her own trail, raising the most beautiful baby, her own little Wise One. While Rosemarie may doubt my way, however, she can certainly have no doubt that I love her or that I am always here for her. We are closer now than we have ever been.

In basketball, Dylan and I have shared a most special bond. Although we have trained together since he was 4 and even though we have spent nearly 24 hours of every day together since he entered high school as both my student and my best player, he also is not me. He has his own dreamquest to pursue, his own voice to heed.

As a father, though, who worked hard to raise kids who would be independent, loving and strong, I feel blessed that my children are so much more aware of their own divine voices than I was when I was their age. They also have the courage I lacked as a child to stand up to authority (usually me) from time to time to fight for their own vision. ***Now, that they are grown, you finally have the time to tell this tale.***

What it All Means

My accident was no accident, it was on purpose and for a purpose. It was written with forethought into my divine plan, a kind of escape clause, set up in case my life drifted too far off course…
Which it did.

…a chance to meet my guardian angel, the old painter who is me, to hear through the noise of the illusion and recognize without fear my own voice in the Quetzal, to have faith in that voice and to know its divinity, to know my own, our own, divine origins.

I have a good friend who helps me coach my varsity basketball team. Neal is a wonderful man who is devoted in his Christian way to God.

"God comes to us in many miraculous ways," Neal recently told me before one of our summer practices, "so you know that voice that you hear, that painter, that jaguar, that man you saw as your father in the zapateria, and all those ghosts? You know that's all God, right?"

I do.

Never doubted it for a minute.

I See the Light

From the ghosts along the Boulevard of the Dead, I learned many lessons. Sure, making sense of these lessons has taken all these past twenty years to accomplish and is mounted upon countless discussions with my guardian angel.

We Are Eternal

The most important lesson was the revelation that everything begins with light. In the light we are derived, to the light we return, and, in the light, we are one. In this revelation, in seeing the light, in the knowing of our oneness, we find our immortality and our own divinity. As I romantically instruct my Ghost Warriors in my classroom, on the basketball court, and as I share with my own children at home;

We are all very old, much older than our age. We are as old as the blood that flows through our veins. It is the blood of the Ghost Warriors, those great warriors in history who fought themselves and others each day to do the right thing. The blood of the Ghost Warriors flows through our veins. We are as old as that blood that flows through our veins and older still if we trace the light that shines through our eyes. It is the light of our creator, our shared divine origin which is eternal.

Lessons of the Journey

Important in all of this is that we are all trapped within an evil illusion orchestrated by the Man in Black, the devil. This illusion, this false reality, keeps us from knowing our true light. Only through the Quetzal can we see through these lies and reconnect with God.

In the Panaderia…

I recovered the little boy in me so severely damaged and traumatized by divorce, racism and bullyism. On that very first stop along that Boulevard of the Dead, I retrieved in a warm rush those traumatized fragments of my soul so in need of being saved and, in that same rescue, helped to liberate another hapless soul trapped within his own suffering and guilt. This mutual salvation came as a result of our own empathy for each other's anguish and the recognition of our oneness in the light.

In reuniting with Chris, the most important lesson of the Seven Sacred Aspects was illustrated and brought home to me; the lesson of our Oneness in the light, within the Quetzal. Respect came with the realization that the light that shined from his eyes was the same that shined from my own, that to hurt one is to hurt all and even yourself. Humility arrived with that understanding as well, and the discovery that he and I shined with the same intensity and that neither shined brighter than the other. He and I were of the same light, his tears reflected his own realization of this and awakened that knowledge within me. A sense of Compassion, Chris' own sensitivity to my suffering, came through his own painful revelation that we are all the same light and that we are thus all one. In Chris, in his tears, I found also my own compassion and empathy conquer the anger and resentment that had crippled me for so long. There was Truth in our innate knowledge of our oneness, Honesty in our intent, Unconditional Love found simply because of our oneness in the light, and the resulting Wisdom in this new awareness we shared.

In Dona Julia's Peluqueria…

I was reconnected with my passions and the dreams of my childhood, the dreams that, like the old painter and the jade jaguar, I had blocked out and learned to forget. As I now believe that our dreams and our passions are divinely channeled mandates for our missions on Earth, I understand that my visit with Dona Julia, the blind barber and storyteller who could see through the illusion of the Man in Black's material illusion into the infinite potential that is all of ours to manifest, was a thing of destiny, a true blessing and a call to my own action.

On The Pagaro Bridge...

The old painter helped me to hear my own voice within the noise of the illusion. There are so many voices in our lives, the voices of our friends, family and those who call themselves enemies. They are the voices of those lost in the illusion or, even worse, in control of it. Confused in this ruckus is our own voice, the voice of our truth, the voice of God within us. Know this voice, tune out the rest, and, I believe, we are lead to what Coehlo calls our personal legend, our dreams, our purpose in life, to our meaning and fulfillment.

Happiness and true fulfillment are possibilities in life, but they are achieved through courage, by boldly singling out that divine voice which is our own and then bravely and faithfully following its call. Living out our dreams, fulfilling our purpose, realizing our highest potentials are the keys to happiness. These things must be fought for. Those who do not fight forfeit their dreams and are forced to hope only for peace of mind. The dreamquest is the revolution; one we fight for the liberation of our very souls. It is a matter of eternal life and eternal death.

Heaven or Hell.

It takes a warrior to be bold and to stand up against the voices of the lie which attack us every day of our lives. The illusion is very powerful, a projection embedded, I believe, into our very DNA, its software supported by mechanisms and instruments of deception woven deeply into the very fabric and infrastructures of our surrounding cultures.

Again, another subject for another book.

It is a malevolent force we must battle everyday - doubtful, fearful and chiding voices we must fight to ignore all the time, for their influence runs so deep within us.

The Man in Black, this fallen angel whose full story, also, will be documented in my next book, knows the human condition well. He knows our physical and spiritual addiction to the illusion – Hell, he is the nasty pusher who hooked us on it over the course of thousands of years, he is the architect of that lie.

Inside our heads, the voices of the illusion, of the lies that most of us have invested our faith in, work on us constantly, bombarding us with guilt and fears, making us feel selfish or unworthy for pursuing the divine paths we were destined to walk, holding us back from our destinies. Dreams never seem to come true without the illusion coming down hard upon us, as the tremors of fear, insecurities and jealousies founded in the illusion work to hold us back and to stop us from achieving our happiness.

Heeding your own voice is the only way to make your dreams come true.

Only by courageously taking hold of our dreams and destinies, I believe, can we expose the lies of the Man in Black, give hope to those around us, and inspire people to see through the illusion into the light, to their highest potential, to their own dreams and purpose in life.

Looking over that bridge into that river of doomed humanity, I understood innately, if not yet intellectually, that my choice in the life I would soon return to would be between following my own voice to Heaven or the lies that would doom me and others to Hell. That assignment to Hell, to be sure, would not have been the result of any deed done bad, as defined, of course, by those codes of morality manufactured by the lie itself, but by our own addiction to the illusion of the Man in Black, who is not empowered by our love but by our fears and who becomes more powerful in his quest to be more God-like through the collection of souls he enslaves within that physical and spiritual addiction to his deception. The sin is not in actions defined as good or bad or right and wrong but in becoming irretrievably immersed in the darkness of his lies. It really is, I believe now, a battle of good versus evil, in which the Man in Black plots to overthrow God.

In a Field…

I saw my daughter, a little girl in garlands, the Wise One. Seeing her here was not only a peek into the future but also a review of the divine plan I had signed on for in the spirit world before I was even born, when I chose, as we all do, the life and life choices I would live.

That vision was a divine heads up of the elevated level of responsibility and accountability I would have to rise to in the life I was soon to return to. No longer would I be able to indulge myself in shameless self-destruction. Now, it would not only be my own soul on the line but the salvation of two others on the way.

At the La Reina...

From my favorite seat I saw the forest from the trees and found meaning and purpose to the beginning, middle and end to my life.

At the Basketball Court...

Reunited with my first love, Henrietta, I found and retrieved a fragment of my soul still hiding out, still traumatized by the guilt of not being there for my father.

In Tia Maria's Kitchen...

I rediscovered that the art of healing comes from a place of unconditional love, a place of just because. For, as she reminded me, the only reward for service is more service.

At the Corner...

A little old lady, I hurt as a boy, found her father in Heaven and led me to my own.

In a Zapateria...

I saw my father and my whole life was brought to a full and sacred circle. There, my entire life magically made sense, my purpose for living, my mission on Earth suddenly became so clear to me. I was from the very beginning, and of my own divine choosing, meant to paint the world blue, whether in a classroom or with a book, to educate, enlighten, and to inspire people to see beyond the illusion, to connect with the divine and to reach out and experience their own limitless potential in life, to embark on their own glorious dreamquests.

Before my father, I became, for the most part, whole again. Looking in that mirror, I felt most of the fragmented pieces of my soul return to me in a warm and exhilarating rush. Most important, I discovered that my guardian angel, he, who, all along, since the days of my childhood and even before, guided me, protected me and whispered to me divine messages, was in fact me all along.

My nagual and power animal guide, the jade jaguar who, like the old painter, was always there as a reflection of my strength. He was also a symbol of the courage it would take to fight for my dreams.

To the Maya, the jaguar served as liaison between the living and the dead and as a companion in the spirit world. No wonder, then, that the jaguar was there to guide me along the Boulevard of the Dead. The jaguar was always there to protect me and watch over me. Today, the jaguar's presence is all about me; hanging around my neck as a pendant and as statuettes on my fireplace. Oprah Winfrey once directed a television audience to always heed "nature's alarms," the feelings that naturally warn us if someone or something is a threat to us. For me, it is the jaguar's growl sounding off in my head, a variety of tones that tell me if something is good or bad, right or wrong, dangerous or safe.

Not long ago, outside of Tucson, a news story broke about the intentional and criminal killing of Macho B, then the last known jaguar in the U.S. As the jaguar is my spirit guide, it was a story, of course, that resonates deep within me and my friend, Jake

"They're killing off the jaguars, Pep," Jake told me recently," at a time when the world needs the jaguar most."

"Who are they?" I asked.

"They are your Man in Black, bad people, evil guys. Be the jaguar, Pep. There's not many of you left. Fight and paint the world blue."

OLD PAINTER'S GALLERY 6

RAINBOW WAY MEDITATION

How can we connect with the Quetzal so as to better recognize our own voice, be stirred by our calling and venture boldly forth to pursue our purpose on Earth? How can we finally break free from this illusion we know to be enslaving us?

There is a way.

The Comanche Medicine Man in shades told us that it was as simple as one and two. On one, he connected his index finger on his right hand with his thumb and, on two, he did the same with his left. "It was that simple," he shared, "to achieve an altered state of consciousness."

Meditation is the key. Finding a quiet haven, a favorite place, free of distraction that allows us to travel within, to sift through the multitude of conflicting voices chattering in our heads, the noise cluttering our minds, so that we can eventually immerse ourselves into the Quetzal, feel God and hear our own divine voices.

A disciplined practice of meditation, at least twice a day, for me in the morning and at night, works to still the mind and to journey inward where our truth awaits. Meditation is a powerful, life-changing tool, which becomes even more effective when practiced consistently.

There are many meditative styles, several pathways to a calm and still mind. Anthony and myself are most familiar and comfortable with the Rainbow Way, taught by the Comanche Medicine Man at his Traditional Indian Medicine seminars. I share with you here, how it was taught to us.

After purifying our auras with sage, the Medicine Man in shades asked the spirits of God's light to protect us, commanding all those spirits that were not of God's light to leave. Then he spoke prayers of gratitude to the Four Directions, North, South, East and West.

The Medicine Man in shades proceeded to have all of us inhale and exhale, each exhalation blowing the noise and clutter from our minds. Once this was done and we sat in peace, our index fingers connected with our thumbs, he guided us through the rainbow of power spots (chakra) along our bodies that, once opened, would help us achieve an altered state that would align us with, what Pep and I call, the Quetzal.

"See and feel the color RED at your groin," the Medicine Man began, "Feel the color RED radiating bright and strong. This is the color RED. This is the color of your PASSION.

We imagined the color red glowing radiant from our groins. We felt and saw the color red, the color of our passion.

"See and feel the color ORANGE at your stomach," he continued, "Feel the color ORANGE radiating bright and strong. This is the color ORANGE. This is the color of your EMOTION.

We imagined the color orange glowing radiant from our stomach. We felt and saw the color orange, the color of our emotion.

"See and feel the color YELLOW at your solar plexus," he continued, "Feel the color YELLOW radiating bright and strong. This is the color YELLOW. This is the color of your INTELLECT.

We imagined the color yellow glowing radiant from our solar plexus. We felt and saw the color yellow, the color of our intellect.

"See and feel the color GREEN at your chest," he continued, "Feel the color GREEN radiating bright and strong. This is the color GREEN. This is the color of your FREEDOM.

We imagined the color green glowing radiant from our chests. We felt and saw the color green, the color of our freedom.

"See and feel the color BLUE at your throat," he continued, "Feel the color BLUE radiating bright and strong. This is the color BLUE. This is the color of COMMUNICATION.

We imagined the color blue glowing radiant from our throats. We felt and saw the color blue, the color of our ability to communicate.

"See and feel the color VIOLET at your third eye," he continued, "Feel the color VIOLET radiating bright and strong. This is the color VIOLET. This is the color of your YOU.

We imagined the color VIOLET glowing radiant from our third eye. We felt and saw the color violet, the color of us, who we were.

"See and feel the color WHITE at your crown," he continued, "Feel the color WHITE radiating bright and strong. This is the color WHITE. This is the color of your Connection with the divine.

We imagined the color white glowing radiant from our crowns. We felt and saw the color white, the color of our connection with God, the very umbilical cord to the Quetzal.

"See and feel the color GOLD above you," he continued, "Feel the color GOLD radiating bright and strong. This is the color GOLD. This is the color of God.

We imagined the color gold glowing radiant above us. We felt and saw the color gold, the color of God.

Once he guided us through the rainbow of power spots, the Medicine Man said, "You are now in an altered state of consciousness. Now, you can go anywhere, meet your guardian angels, talk to God and find answers."

From this launching point, Pep and I have since embarked on many journeys together, engaged in countless conversations about the meaning of life, found our peace, our truth and our voices in the Quetzal.

Indeed, in the Quetzal, Pep reunited with his Ever Girl.

AFFIRMATIONS

A few years ago, my sister introduced me to a woman who was known to be a powerful shamanic healer from Great Britain. While I could find very little regarding this woman online, the little information I was able to dig up suggested that she had quietly been enjoying great success advising leaders in the corporate world to personal, professional and spiritual success and growth.

My sister was going through her own process of reinvention. No longer a journalist, she was making an entrepreneurial dive into the world of entertainment as a producer. Now, at this precarious time, she swore by this shaman who she credited with reawakening the goddess within and inspiring her to dream great things again.

My sister was very interested in a script I wrote many years before. It was a fantasy adventure rooted in Toltec spirituality and legend entitled, *Aztlan Warriors*.

"Do you still have it?" she emailed me.

"I do," I answered her.

"I think I can sell it, Pep. I really believe that it's time!"

Things really seemed to be taking off. My sister had somehow attached a major actress to my screenplay and we were scheduled to meet with a recently knighted cinematic icon about directing it. As this giant was one of my idols in the industry, I was very nervous about meeting him, let alone getting up in front of him and his partners to act out my entire script. Clearly, this was a potentially huge deal for both my sister and myself. Because of this I consented, for my sister's peace of mind and because there was nothing to lose, to do a session with her shamanic advisor.

"We have to be right and at our best when we go into this meeting, Pep," my sister explained, "this woman is amazing and she's changed my life. She'll help to balance your energy and dispel any residual negativity before the meeting."

Sounded good to me.

While the deal with the legendary director eventually fell through, the meeting with this shaman would prove quite meaningful and would further validate the lessons of the Boulevard of the Dead.

Shamanic Journey

The shaman and I met twice in two days. At our first session, we sat for a prayer before the big meeting with the great director and, the second time, we met at my sister's home the next day for a full-on soul retrieval.

The soul retrieval began with me laying on the floor while the shaman sang out prayers and shook her rattle about me, calling upon the spirits of God's light to surround us with loving energy and to guide her on her journey to find whatever traumatized fragments of my soul might still be lost or trapped within the spirit world so that she might set them free and complete whatever healing still needed to be done. **Most of this was already achieved on the Boulevard of the Dead. Still, there were a couple soul fragments left to be liberated.**

She then lay beside me on the floor, making physical contact with me with her foot. For about a half hour we both laid there in silence as she journeyed into the spirit world on my behalf. When she returned, she shared with me her visions and the affirmation that my fragmented souls had finally been set free to join the whole of who I was. I recount her journey here only as it is a validation of my own journey down the Boulevard of the Dead, which, as I see it, was its own mission of soul retrieval.

The shaman journeyed deep into the spirit world, assisted by my jaguar spirit guide, to find a long, lost piece of me, a sad little boy still trapped in the bedroom of my Sherman Oaks apartment, watching television and drawing on my bed. A few feet from the boy was a dark closet, from which a mysterious Man in Black would occasionally stick out his head to look upon his young captive. This boy, traumatized by his parent's divorce, hid from the world in his bedroom which was guarded by the Devil himself.

Radiating a bright white ring of light throughout the room, she rendered the Man in Black powerless and set the boy free. Hadn't I set this same little boy free years before at that last stop on the Boulevard of the Dead? The splinters of a shattered soul are sometimes in the multitudes and often so infinitesimal that they are difficult to find. The Man in Black is relentless and will take whatever parts of our souls he can steal, no matter how small. There are probably still several little boys lost somewhere in that fog along that Boulevard of the Dead, like POWs left behind, waiting to be saved. No matter how insignificant the shard may seem, its weight upon the whole of one's spirit is heavy and indispensable. The spirit must be whole.

With this boy released from his prison, the shaman proceeded, still in the company of my jaguar, to a place where she met my father. My father, dressed in the robes of a Mayan High Priest, still watched over me, she said, although he made an effort to stay out of my life now and not bother me as much. After Dylan's birth, I didn't feel my father's presence in my life as much as I once had. His presence in my life now, the shaman said, was more about his own process of letting go of the idea that I was still weak and still in need of being taken care of.

"Pep is strong now," she told him, 'He is a warrior, an artist, a shaman like you, painting the world blue as you directed. He doesn't need to be taken care of. Go now, to Heaven. You are released from this world."

Apparently, my father felt guilt even in the afterlife about leaving his boy with no father. Although I idolized Horace and while Horace was a wonderful and caring stepfather, my father felt that his boy still needed him.

Finally, on a high peak, the shaman saw me also in the garb of a Mayan High Priest, a warrior-priest actually, holding a staff.

"I saw you there, Pep," she told me, "you were powerful like your father, with a jade staff in your hands and a jaguar nearby. You were a healer, a shaman yourself."

To this person, she told me that a new spirit animal would be introduced, to guide me alongside my jaguar. This was the otter.

"The otter comes to you, Pep," she later explained to me, "to teach you how to smile more."

At that, I actually did smile. I have always loved otters.

"You're ready," she told me, "you're ready to come out of hiding and stake your powerful claim to the title of Warrior Priest!"

You have come out of hiding, Pep. You are the Warrior Priest. You are...

Ghost Warrior!

EPILOGUE:
CONVERSATIONS WITH MY ANGEL

Over the years, my guardian angel, the old painter, that deepest and highest aspect of who I am, and I have maintained a running dialogue on almost every subject in the universe; including the nature and purpose of life, reality and God. He really is me – we are one and the same – he is that highest aspect of who I am, and I can only connect with him or that aspect of me when I am living in the Quetzal.

From our lengthy discourses, I have been able to conclude for myself that there is a God, a creator, masculine or feminine or both and that there is goodness, light and love in the ever-expanding universe. It is through my angel that I hear my own voice in the Quetzal and in that do I hear God. The old painter and I have agreed to write more detailed books based on our discourses and divine revelations.

On the Man in Black and his mechanisms of deception.

As I know God, I know that there is also evil. There is a devil, a Man in Black. I know him to be an enemy of God, one who has fallen, who would usurp God's place, who has already tried and failed. This Man in Black does not want to be like God, he wants to be God.

This Man in Black is our enemy and, make no mistake, we are at war with him.

He does not want us to know the light that we really are, or the truth of our unlimited and divine potential which we can find in that light-sonic frequency I know to be the Quetzal, or the God vibration. He is a collector, a harvester of souls. He wants ours. He wants yours.

The Man in Black keeps us from the Quetzal, blocks our connection with this frequency with a cacophony of lies. Certainly, the Man in Black has cast a spell upon us. It is an Illusion, a projection so manipulative and malevolent that it is, I repeat, ingeniously embedded into the software of our very DNA, the foods we consume, the air we breathe, the cultural values within which we are assimilated and the noise that deafens us to our own divine calling.

How, then, do we set ourselves forever free from this Illusion? The Quetzal is our only hope for salvation. How do we connect and find our voice in this frequency? Alas, the answer to this and other questions are not to be fully answered here. Here, it is enough only that the questions are raised.

This book was about your journey along the Boulevard of the Dead.

The Man in Black and the Mechanisms of Deception

This book was intended only to chronicle the revelations of my trek along the Boulevard of the Dead, while retrieving the fragmented pieces of my own soul. It is a documentation of a kind of vision quest, where I found myself and came to terms finally with my purpose, my mission. Through the telling of this tale it is also my hope to challenge my readers to take up the crusade to find their own voices and fight to discover then live out their own purpose.

In my next book...

Our next book.

I will concentrate all my efforts on exposing this illusion, the Man in Black who designed it and all the mechanisms that support the lie around us. What is the Man in Black's purpose in enslaving mankind within this malevolent network of lies? What exactly are the Mechanisms of Deception woven into the fabric of worldly cultures that keep us chained and in check within the illusion?

I will also explore a lifestyle conducive to living life in the Quetzal, which would thus, fend off all the fears, guilt, doubts, insecurities, and other dark ghosts of the illusion so designed to stop us from connecting with God and living out the Creator's will. No one knows more about being victimized by the illusion than myself...unless, it is you.

I am not a Zen master, a guru, or a Toltec sorcerer (although, in a previous life, I was a Mayan high priest). I am a warrior and a master only of my own experience and of the truths I have come to have faith in. I am far from perfect. In my 50's, I am evolving still.

Sometimes the learning comes easy and sometimes it is painful. It is difficult still, no matter how self-aware, to let go of the lies we have been conditioned to cling to and in which we have invested so much of our faith in for so long. The truth, however, is the truth no matter what and I believe that we are all blessed at birth with the ability to recognize it. This blessing is ours no matter the environments we are raised in. I am indeed, an imperfect channel of God's truth but it wouldn't be the first time our creator chose the most unlikely of instruments to communicate his message.

It is as a Ghost Warrior that I fight every day. Sometimes I win, sometimes I lose, and sometimes, as is common within the illusion of life, I forget I'm in a war altogether. But, in a war I am as are we all, whether we know it or not. It is a war I now know to be for the salvation of our very souls.

It is as a Ghost Warrior that I fight everything that I know to be real so that I may recognize and embrace God's truth within the Quetzal. I have faith more and more that the voice I know to be my own, the voice of my angel (which is me) is the voice of God speaking out to me.

It is as a Ghost Warrior that I fight to ignore the lies of my past, the labels and the pressure of petty human drama. It is too easy to get lost, to believe the lies and let the Man in Black win. It takes a Ghost Warrior to rise to the challenge every day, to find a new reason every day to keep that link with God and fend off the Devil.

It takes a bold Ghost Warrior to stand up to the Mechanisms of Deception and live our dreams. Certainly, I fight the illusion still and finding a quiet place for myself; whether in my darkened bedroom (for at long last, I now know that it is okay to live life in my head), shooting baskets and dribbling alone on my driveway or at a park, sitting on a rock overlooking the Monterey Bay, meditating in Ojai, or finding a clearing within an emerald forest of old redwoods; any place that allows me the freedom to live life in my head and find my own voice in the Quetzal is essential to saving my soul. I paint the world blue with the legacy I leave for my children, with my coaching on the basketball court, my teaching, my stories and, I hope, with this book.

The first of many.

It takes a Warrior of Mind, Body and Spirit, a Ghost Warrior, to fight against the illusion. May you also be a brave Warrior, may you finally see through the Man in Black's illusion, may you break free, find your passion, do God's Will and save your soul.

Until we meet in the Quetzal.

GHOST WARRIORS OF THE QUETZAL
(As told by the Old Painter)

The QUETZAL is the light-sonic vibration
that connects us with the DIVINE.
We are WARRIORS of MIND, BODY and SPIRIT

We are WARRIORS of MIND
because we fight to learn

We are WARRIORS of BODY
because we fight to keep our bodies strong

We are WARRIORS of SPIRIT
because we fight to keep alive The SEVEN SACRED ASPECTS

which are:

1.RESPECT,
2.HUMILITY,
3.COMPASSION,
4.TRUTH,
5.HONESTY,
6.UNCONDITIONAL LOVE
7.WISDOM.

1. RESPECT
comes with the realization that the LIGHT
shining in our eyes is the same LIGHT
that shines in the eyes of all men.

That same LIGHT
energizes and unites all living things

RESPECT
comes with the recognition and the revelation
that we are all ONE
within the QUETZAL

2. HUMILITY
comes with the knowing that we all shine
with the same intensity
and no one man shines brighter
than the next

We are all born of the LIGHT
and ONE within the QUETZAL

Each of us is ALIVE
with our DIVINE PLAN,
PURPOSE and DREAMS

Each of us equal
and with equal PURPOSE
within the QUETZAL
and within
GOD'S MYSTERY

3. COMPASSION
means that we are sensitive
to the SUFFERINGS of others.
To hurt ONE is to hurt ourselves

To LOVE ourselves and others
is to LOVE ALL

4. TRUTH
means that we are HONEST with others
Through our WORD and our INTENT

5. HONESTY
means we are TRUTHFUL
with our own INTENT
TRUTHFUL with ourselves
to the QUETZAL
to our own VOICE
and to our
DIVINE PURPOSE

6. UNCONDITIONAL LOVE
means that we LOVE ourselves
and others simply because
we are all the same bright
and DIVINE source

We LOVE just BECAUSE

7. WISDOM
is the knowledge we gain
from the mistakes we make
along the path to discovering the LIGHT
that burns within us

As GHOST WARRIORS we FIGHT the GHOSTS
of our PAST, of our FEARS,
and the LIES of the DEVIL'S ILLUSION
so that we might ultimately KNOW with FAITH
who we really are...
the CHILDREN OF GOD

GHOST WARRRIORS
are not necessarily always
CONQUERORS.
We are WARRIORS,
for we FIGHT

We FIGHT everyday
to do the RIGHT THING
as WARRIORS of
MIND, BODY and SPIRIT

It takes a WARRIOR of MIND
to FIGHT to LEARN,
to keep the MIND sharp
to read, to grow
and expand the intellect
It is so much easier
to allow our blessed BODIES,
the temples that house our souls,
to rot and fall into decay

It takes a WARRIOR of BODY
to keep our BODIES strong,
to eat the right foods and to exercise
It would be so easy to allow
our blessed connection with SPIRIT
to rot and fall into decay
to become lost within the LIE
To forget our everlasting ONENESS
within the QUETZAL
It takes a GHOST WARRIOR to FIGHT
through the ILLUSIONS of
PETTY HUMAN DRAMA

It takes a GHOST WARRIOR
to BATTLE
through the ADDICTIONS
of our EGOS
and SEE THROUGH
the MATERIAL
INTO THE LIGHT
that WE ARE

INTO the QUETZAL
Through the QUETZAL
GOD has BLESSED us all
with a VISION
of OUR PURPOSE

And that is...
OUR DREAM

It is a DREAM
to be FOUGHT FOR,
A DREAM to be LIVED

By living this DREAM
we do
GOD'S MYSTERIOUS WORK

We become DIVINE WARRIORS
delivering mankind from the
DARKNESS
of the DEVIL'S ILLUSION
in which we are ENSLAVED,
from the LIES
by which we are DECEIVED
and in which we have mistakenly
placed our FAITH

As GHOST WARRIORS,
we boldly venture
into the TRUTH
of the QUETZAL
and into the LIGHT that WE ARE

It takes a GHOST WARRIOR to FIGHT
to do the RIGHT THING

It takes a GHOST WARRIOR to FIGHT for the DREAM

In this DREAM
We find our PURPOSE
and this PURPOSE is DIVINE

These BATTLES
require that a GHOST WARRIOR
be STRONG of MIND, healthy of BODY, and
CONNECTED to SPIRIT

The SCARS from these BATTLES
will not be MANIFEST on our FLESH
But, instead, SEARED
into our HEARTS and SOULS

These BATTLES are FOUGHT
on SPIRITUAL BATTLEFIELDS

As GHOST WARRIORS
We are very OLD.
We are as OLD as the BLOOD
that flows through our veins

It is
The BLOOD of all
the great GHOST WARRIORS
who have come before us

It is their BLOOD
that flows through our veins.
Indeed, we are very OLD.

Older still,
To trace the SOURCE
of the LIGHT
that SHINES through our EYES

It is the LIGHT
Of CREATION
that binds us ALL
and CONNECTS us ALL
To GOD.

PEP TORRES

PEP TORRES is a visionary artist, writer, storyteller, motivational speaker, performer, teacher and a successful high school basketball coach.

In constant communication with his guardian angel, an old painter he met in a near-death experience more than twenty years ago, Torres believes that he was put on Earth to paint the world blue, enlighten, and heal people through the stories he tells.

Through his unique and entertaining style, Torres heals the broken heart and inspires the warrior within to once again fight for the life we all dream for ourselves. In this, Torres lives out his own dreams and realizes his own divine purpose. In this, also, he obeys his own divine mandate to paint the world blue.

Printed in the United States
By Bookmasters